AF478634

Storytelling in Organizations

# Storytelling in Organizations

## From Theory to Empirical Research

Anna Linda Musacchio Adorisio

First published 2009 by
PALGRAVE MACMILLAN

Palgrave Macmillan in the UK is an imprint of Macmillan Publishers Limited, registered in England, company number 785998, of Houndmills, Basingstoke, Hampshire RG21 6XS.

Palgrave Macmillan in the US is a division of St Martin's Press LLC, 175 Fifth Avenue, New York, NY 10010.

Palgrave Macmillan is the global academic imprint of the above companies and has companies and representatives throughout the world.

Palgrave® and Macmillan® are registered trademarks in the United States, the United Kingdom, Europe and other countries.

ISBN-13: 978–0–230–23068–2 hardback

This book is printed on paper suitable for recycling and made from fully managed and sustained forest sources. Logging, pulping and manufacturing processes are expected to conform to the environmental regulations of the country of origin.

A catalogue record for this book is available from the British Library.

A catalog record for this book is available from the Library of Congress.

10   9   8   7   6   5   4   3   2   1
18   17   16   15   14   13   12   11   10   09

Printed in the United States of America

*I dedicate my work to the people to whom stories matter.*

# Contents

# List of Illustrations and Table

## Illustrations



## Table

# Foreword by David Boje

Anna Linda Musacchio developed new insights into the field of storytelling. It is a field complicated by many definitions. Some treat story and narrative as just the same thing. Most of the management domain is rather confused on this point. My personal view is that storytelling is a combination of narratives stuck in past-new, living stories with fuzzy beginning and no end in sight, and the antenarratives that shape the future. It is important to treat storytelling in its complexity. Anna Linda has taken the time to spell out how Russian Formalism developed its approaches to narrative. Most of the people in management do not have the time to revise Russian Formalism, European and American Structuralism, then sort through post-structuralism.

I believe the contribution of this book is in developing a theory of storytelling that is rooted in praxis (knowledge + action, as Paulo Freire would say). Storytelling is very much a social practice, one where official narratives dominate living stories.

It is Anna Linda's study of the everyday, living story-life of Wells Fargo that is so very revealing. The novelty of this banking conglomerate stands out in the study of everyday life. We get an up close and personal look at how an official narrative is branded onto, and dominates the living story, and replaces all narrative history of the branded banks.

I went on several of the interviews, and watched Anna Linda, do her storytelling research. She has a way of noticing the importance of a pause, a silence, an hesitation in the voice. There are these moments captured in her presence, in her transcripts, in her analysis – that richly develop.

The book itself is on the storytelling, on how the storytelling is performed. It is all about the fragments of official narrative, and the living story (as I call it).

The book is about the relation of consolidated and rough stories. A consolidated narrative reduces living story to a blueprint. The rough stories are more living, more morphing, more spontaneous and alive. The two are in the same storytelling space. There are these stories such as "The Tower", "Anthony's Miracle", and "Frank was not a banker" that turn out to be pivotal in the analysis. They each reveal an emotional attachment. In my view, this illustrates what Bakhtin calls emotive-ethical. It is an emotional ethical connection, an interplay of two discourses, and it courses through the body and through being human. So much emotion is restricted, edited out of professional life, out of being bankers and customers. The emotive-ethical is an important analysis. It may be the key to unlock the tangle of banking, its mess-making, in the global recession. Consumption and banking are emotional, not just rational, and this has ethical importance. I think what is going on in Anna Linda's work is that there is an answerability revealed in a pause, an extra breath.

Consolidated narratives are socially organized and socially plotted. Rough stories, on the other hand, are more akin to what I have called antenarratives. It is important to say here, that the pole of rough storytelling does not always coincide exactly with antenarrative. Antenarrative covers both what exists before narrative and counternarrative. As Anna Linda explains, "counternarratives can be very organized and structured as well, and follow the same patterns of narratives" (p. 132). Her work focuses on antenarrative in the notation that excludes counternarrative.

The core of Anna Linda's research contribution must be detected, in fact, in the recognition of the ambivalence of storytelling acts, which witness a constant movement between the consolidated, socially plotted narratives, and the rough and unfinished fragments (antenarrative). Life is in between and social organization is in between narrative fossils and what is rough and wild story.

The book, then is this exploration of interplay between consolidated narrative and rough story. For example, there are more rough fragments in the accounts of the bankers of the former First National Bank of Dona Ana. The bankers of First National tell First National now. And as Anna Linda points out, "it is an account of the past made now, while the Wells Fargo bankers tell Wells Fargo in the same moment". This idea that the account of the present I made now in expression, in storytelling, is an important contribution. It reveals that narrative without context is a kind of cultural ignorance. In being able to sort context implications into the telling and listening, storyteller's develop the kind of competence which in Walter

Benjamin days is lost, dead, or just a forgotten skill of storytelling in modern organizations.

It was my distinct pleasure and honor to work with Anna Linda Musacchio in her research, to go on field adventures into banking in the Wild West of New Mexico. It was awesome to see her extend Russian Formalism, incorporate new ideas of consolidated and rough and wild telling, and give new insight into banking. It is a good read, and a book that has a lasting contribution. – David M. Boje

# Acknowledgments

I want to thank Professor Jedlowski who supported this project when accepting to become the supervisor of my thesis. Who knows the story, is aware of the fact that this work wouldn't have been written without this consent.

My gratitude goes equally to Professor Boje who has supervised me during my empirical research at New Mexico State University and has taught me how powerful stories are.

I have to thank Professor Loveland for opening the door into this wonderful story.

Finally I want to thank John Papen who has been of extraordinary help and who is a great storyteller.

# Introduction

This book is about storytelling in organizations, a notion that encompasses both the stories that are told within organizations by its members and the stories that organizations create in the form of official speeches, brochures, advertisement and so on.

My empirical research aims at studying these phenomena in the context of a US Southwestern bank and its successors in the town of Las Cruces, New Mexico.

A narrative study of organizations is necessarily a multidisciplinary endeavor. Narrative studies draw on very distant fields: literary criticism; philosophy of language; pragmatics of communication; sociolinguistics, just to name a few. Various and alternative fields of reference equally inform the organizational domain: economics, sociology, anthropology, psychology and communication studies as well.

The privileged angle of analysis of my study is that of the sociology of culture and sociology of communication in terms of studies that privileged the analysis of the role of communication and culture in the interpretation of social life.

The work stands at the cross-roads of two different traditions: on the one hand that of the studies of communicational practices in everyday life, developed in Italy and present here in the interpretation provided by Paolo Jedlowski, my PhD thesis advisor in Lugano; on the other hand that of narrative studies in the organizational domain, developed in the Anglo-Saxon world and present here in the interpretation provided by David Boje, with whom I have performed my empirical research during a visiting fellowship at New Mexico State University.

This work is the result of a research path that has been evolving and unfolding over the years in different, but not conflicting, directions. Moreover the empirical research performed and the interviews with the bankers have played a significant role in the shaping of the research focus itself.

The presentation of the work witnesses different stages of the research, and the different theoretical approaches considered.

The initial idea was that of studying the relation between narrative practices and decision-making processes. The paradigm would have been a socio-constructionist one. Narrative practices would have represented a sort of sense-making device for decision-making.

The more I researched on narrative definitions, the more I felt unsatisfied with such interpretation; moreover the richness of the material collected made me aware of the amazing complexity and the multiple functions that storytelling performs.

Storytelling is one of the most common sense-making devices, but in ths book I will explore alternative functions of storytelling and I will problematize this issue.

In the Chapter 1 will provide an outline of different interpretations of narrative related concepts, starting from the structural interpretation provided by Russian Formalists, to socio-constructionist views of storytelling and to phenomenological and postmodern interpretations.

It is already at this level that preference will be accorded to authors such as Ricoeur or Bakhtin who have problematized the concept of narrative, allowing for the emergence of a dynamic and dialogic dimension.

While the first chapter investigates the concept of narrative on a more general level, the second chapter is devoted to narrative studies in the organizational domain: how it was possible for narrative and communicational research to enter the organizational domain and what have been the most influential works on my research. Boje's published articles of 1991 and 1995 and his articulation of the concept of storytelling organization have performed a primary role in this sense. Decision-making and narrative will be treated as a separate and final section of the second chapter.

Chapter 3 will represent a connection chapter that will summarize the relevant concepts and pose the questions arising from them. It is with the empirical research, treated in the second part of the work in

Chapters 4 and 5, that the research will take its turn. Chapter 4 will outline the research methodology and methods used in a personal and narrative fashion. The research performed is similarly informed by previous research experiences, such as that of Boje, and by the direct application of theoretical concepts that are, from time to time, relevant.

Chapter 5 contains the edited excerpts of different material sources: interviews with bankers, books written on the topic, brochures, newsletters, archival information and direct observation. This material will be presented in an edited narrative manner following, in seven sections, an historical development: from the origins of the bank, to the life at the bank, the acquisitions and the new life. It will be commented on briefly using the theory stemming from the first part of the work and it will sketch further questions arising from the research experience and from the expression in the excerpts themselves. Chapter 6, similarly to Chapter 3, is a connection chapter, which summarizes the second part to the light of the questions and problems that will be treated in the last part of the book.

In the final chapters we return to the theory and a further refinement of it. Chapter 7 represents the further refinement of the research in theoretical articulation: Bakhtin and Ricoeur will be reconsidered, together with some of Boje's and Jedlowski's articulations. The work of these scholars will meet to articulate the line of analysis of the work. This is the main chapter: the novelty of the work and its findings are presented in it.

Chapter 8 represents what is left of the initial interest for decision-making: different understanding of the phenomena will be outlined through the revision of different normative and descriptive accounts of decision models. The chapter will articulate this in the line of a proposal rather than in an answer to initial question. The proposal will be that of studying decision-making as part of everyday life in organizations, starting from the experience of the people involved in these processes and using the complexity that the narrative/antenarrative lens can provide us with.

Finally, a short conclusion will summarize the work and will underline its specificity within the field of narrative inquiries about organizations.

# Part I

# Studying Stories: A Theoretical Background

# 1
# Stories, Narratives and Storytelling Practices

To provide a nonambiguous definition of narrating seems to be quite a complex endeavor. There are multiple interpretations of the phenomenon, as well as countless scholars who have provided narrative definitions according to their epistemological foundations and the purposes of their analyses.

In the first chapter I will pull together some of these interpretations and highlight some of the key concepts concerning a narrating definition that can be useful ground for the second part of the book – where we will see them at play in a specific organizational context. The first chapter stands at the crossroads of different disciplines as narrative analysis, originally conceived in the literary criticism tradition, has over time acquired significant importance in the social sciences – informed by the insights of disciplines such as philosophy of language, pragmatics of communication or sociolinguistics, just to name a few.

A distinction must be made between the study of narrative using a structuralist approach, the study of narrative using a sociological approach and the study of narrative using a combination of the sociological approach and insights from postmodern philosophical thought and phenomenologist sensitivity, which will be my approach.

## 1.1   Beyond Fabula and Syzhet?

For a first definition of narrative we can recall the work of literary theorists who were interested in narratology (Todorov, 1965, 1986), that is to say the analysis of the structures of narrative literary texts, the main question for them being: what are the possible basic structure of narratives? "What is narrative per se? What properties must a text have to be called a narrative, and what properties disqualify it?" asks Chatman (1984, p. 258), within the intellectual debate that grew out of the symposium "Narrative: the Illusion of Sequence", held at the University of Chicago on 26–28 October 1979.

Vladimir Propp's thorough analysis of Russian Folktales (Propp, 1928) is a significant example of structuralist endeavor and probably the first contemporary study on narrative analysis. I use the word contemporary in order to distinguish it from the hermeneutic studies of scriptures, which date back to the middle ages. Aristotle's *Poetics* can also be considered a pioneering work in narrative analysis, although my decision is to start with contemporary accounts.

In order to approach the narrative definition given by narratologists we have to start from what it is considered for them to be the key element of every narrative text, that is to say temporal development (Chatman, 1978; Prince, 1982). Every narrative text is characterized by a development, by a set of events following one after the other which are able to signal the passage from one opposite to the other, from an initial to a different final state (often in the form of a conflict). Using the words of two bespoken narratologists, narrative "may be defined as the representation of real or fictive events and situations in a time sequence" (Prince, 1982, p. 1), or can be viewed as "the shift from one equilibrium to another...separated by a period of imbalance" (Todorov, 1986, p. 328). The constant element of narrativity for narratologists seems to be a sort of evolution, a shift that can be related to time sequence.

However, the time of the events does not always correspond to the time of narration, that is to say that the events are presented in narrative in a way that does not always correspond to their chronological evolution.

If we think of certain movies such as *Pulp Fiction* (Tarantino, 1994) where a set of intertwined events is broken down and reassembled in nonlinear sequences, or the French *Irréversible* (Noé, 2002) where the narration is made in reverse to the chronological time sequence of events, we should have no difficulties in understanding such a distinction.

It comes from the Russian Formalist tradition – the distinction between the notion of *Фабула* (*fabula*) indicating the events in their chronological sequence and the notion of *Сюжет* (*syzhet*) indicating the events in the order presented in the text (Tomaševskij, 1975, p. 185). Formalist scholars such as Boris Eichenbaum, Viktor Šklovskij and Boris Tomaševskij have provided great insights into the description of different devices used in literature (flashbacks, frame story, in medias res, parallel, etc.) to construct the *syzhet* (Šklovskij, 1925; Todorov, 1965). If we just think of our personal narrative readings we can find examples of these devices, speaking for myself I can think of the Boccaccio's *Decameron* frame story studied during middle school or the fascinating childhood reading of *One Thousand and One Nights*, or again for parallel *Anna Karenina*, and so on.

The distinction between *fabula* and *syzhet* relies on a diegetic distinction, where diegesis refers to the telling, as opposed to mimesis, which refers to the showing. Diegesis is basically the telling of the story by the narrator, the entering into a created time-space continuum. Each story entails a different time-space continuum and *syzhet* indicates how this time space is manipulated or presented, by the teller. Many narratology terms are also used in film theory as a matter of fact many examples can be made just using the film material. In films, diegesis is sometimes made explicit by the voice of the narrator or by showing the contrast between the "narrative space" and the real situation of the teller.

The formalist distinction between *fabula* and *syzhet* has been assimilated with the distinction between story and discourse, where story is the whole of the narrated events and discourse is the way in which the author has presented them to us.[1]

In the words of formalist narratologists the way events are presented follows specific patterns that although different in each story can nevertheless be assimilated. Similarly to the structural interpretation of myths, formalist narratology emphasizes the structure of every story rather than its always changing material or the contextual aspects under which stories come to be recounted.

In this sense, an interesting and alternative point of view comes from a narratologist named Gérard Genette, who distinguishes between story (*histoire*), discourse (*récit*) and narrative (*narration*) (Genette, 1972). The first term (*histoire*) refers to the events that are the object of a discourse: the signified or narrated content; the second term (*récit*) refers to the utterance of an account of one or a series of events, through which the events are presented, in other words the signifier or the narrative text itself; and the third term (*narration*) refers to the act of telling itself. What is interesting is that as a narratologist he introduces this third instance, even though in his work it is treated as something internal to the text. As Jedlowski argues this is tied to the nature of narratologist's interests which are the logical models working within the texts rather than the narrating as an empirically observable action (Jedlowski, 2000, p. 14). It is the situation of the telling that is outside narratologists' interests while the figure of the storyteller with its sociological presence, as in Walter Benjamin *The Storyteller* (Benjamin, 1936), is actually the focus of my analysis. Genette's distinction is very important as it allows us to bridge narrative theory as conceived in the narratology tradition with the sociological accounts that are the focus of this study.

Returning to Genette's distinction a further element of ambiguity may be generated by the fact that in colloquial French *récit* is more likely to be assimilated with the English acceptation of narrative than to the one of discourse. If I consult the dictionary I find that *récit=relation orale ou écrite de faits vrais ou imaginaries* (Micro, Robert, 2003) is the same as, narrative = spoken or written account of connected events (The New Oxford Dictionary of English, 2003), whereas Genette's narrative (*narration*) refers more to the actual act of telling rather than to the narrative utterance (discourse or text).

It is interesting noticing here that in the organizational domain, scholars have strongly debated on story and narrative definitions: basically every single author has his or her own interpretation of the topic, and uses the terms narrative and story with different acceptations.

My personal focus is on storytelling as a practice inscribed in social relations and for this reason I would insist on the notion of narrating or storytelling instead of talking about stories or narratives. I will put the subject, the narrator, and his or her experience at the center of my analysis. In the narrative analysis of texts performed by Russian Formalists there is no interest for the context in which the text was generated: there is no reference made to the narrator's (author) experience nor to the relation between the author and the reader. Those studies represent, nevertheless, the basis for interpretation of many narrative analysis studies in both communication and organizational research, and for this reason I think it is relevant to discuss them in this work.

The idea for me is that of both envisioning narrating and finding a way to study the phenomenon, where the experience of the people involved could be the center of the analysis.

Whether the result is a story or a narrative is not important, as the separability of the two is questioned. Bakhtin (Bakhtin and Medvedev, 1978, p. 113) was probably the first one to point out that the distinction between *fabula* and *syzhet* is redundant and to affirm that story/*fabula* itself is a form of artistic creation as well as *syzhet*/narrative, (he uses the word plot, which creates further confusion) "even in life we see the story with the eye of the plot" (Bakhtin and Medvedev, 1978, p. 139). This apparently simple consideration entails a radically different understanding of the aforementioned concepts. The idea is that *fabula* itself is not a fixed and atemporal instance. *Fabula* is reconstructed given the context and the current perspective of the narrator, that is to say that not only discourse but also story (if one exists) changes in every account.[2]

There has been an interesting debate between Chatman and Barbara Herrnstein Smith (1981) in which Herrnstein Smith argues "For any particular narrative, there is no single basically story subsisting beneath it but, rather, an unlimited number of other narratives that can be constructed in response to it or perceived as related to it" (Herrnstein Smith, 1981, p. 217).

Herrnstein Smith also relaxed the assumption of two connected events and the beginning, middle, end as the minimum condition for narrativity, proposing a definition of narrative as "someone tells someone else that something happened" (Herrnstein Smith, 1981, p. 228).

On the same line Hannah Arendt (1985, pp. 261–262) argues, "Reality is different from, and more than, the totality of facts and events, which anyhow, is unascertainable." "Who says what is … always tells a story, and in this story the particular facts lose their contingency and acquire some humanly comprehensible meaning."

It is important to clarify here that the problematic relation between a preexisting or independent reality and narration will be solved using Ricoeur's thinking (1983, 1992), which will appear in different sections throughout the work.

The basic idea is that we inhabit a world that has a temporality characterized by a "before" and an "after", as suggested by history or physics, yet it is only our ability to experience the reality that makes this temporality significant for us. Human time for Ricoeur is the place where phenomenological time is reinscribed on cosmological time. Stories articulate this third time, as time becomes human time when it is narrated. Of course each narrative represents an alternative to how experience is temporalized and this is because reality holds a surplus, an excess of sense that shapes stories in unlimited configurations.

In a similar perspective "experience is made or fashioned; it is not encountered, discovered or observed", says Schafer (1992), and again, "introspection does not encounter ready made material" but instead creates those materials according to its current expectations and interpretations (p. 23). "The Self is a kind of telling, it is a telling rather than a teller" (Schafer, 1978, p. 86).

Schafer argues that there is nothing simply there before the various tellings and retellings through which we shape our lives, and this I believe is a good starting point for my work, which goes beyond the *fabula/syzhet* distinction. It must be noticed that although Schafer's citation can be fully inscribed in the postmodern sensitivity ("there is nothing"), Ricoeur's position is not as strong in this sense; there is something before or independent of narration for Ricoeur, but it can be accessible and shaped only through narration. In my study I will adopt Herrnstein Smith's definition "someone tells someone else that something has happened" and amend it with Ricoeur's sensitivity to temporality and experience as the starting point for my analysis.

## 1.2  Narrative time

Such arguments will be revisited, but before doing so I will spend some more time on the notion of time for narrative definitions. I have already talked about the order of the events as presented in the text and the order of the events in the words of formalist/structuralist narratologists. Here I want to talk about the story time (*erzählzeit*) and the discourse/narration time (*erzählte zeit*). It is a distinction, formulated in the forties by Günther Müller, elaborated on by Ricoeur (1983) and which is the object of the three volumes *Time and Narrative.* In this fascinating study the French philosopher asks himself what is the relationship between the time of/within the narratives and the objective notion of time (assuming that the latter exists and is not a "mere illusion, albeit a very persistent one" as suggested by Einstein). In order to answer this question Ricoeur (1983, vol. 3, p. 17) introduces the distinction between cosmological time (time of the world, *temps du monde* in French) and phenomenological time (time of the soul, *temps de l'âme*, in French) that is to say between subjective and objective time as elaborated respectively by Aristotle and Augustine.

Leaving aside the possible aporia between a notion of time as an "attribute of movement" (Aristotle, *Physics*, IV, 11, 2, 10) and a notion of time related to the *"distentio animi"* (Augustine, *Confessions*) the French philosopher provides us with an extremely powerful suggestion for the narrating of organizational life, which is the focus of my study. Is the time of narratives of organizational life the time of the world, the cosmological time of the clock and of the movement of stars or is it the soul time, the phenomenological time, the time of the relevant events of our lives?

Not only Aristotle but also Newton, Leibniz, Husserl and Kant are recalled to attention by Ricoeur's distinction between a notion of time as a priori concept which exists before experience and a notion of intuitive time, as the expression of our inner lived experience and thus invisible time (Ricoeur, 1983, vol. 3, p. 37).

Ricoeur's powerful suggestion stands in the answer, in the identification of a third time, the time of narrative, which is "the inscription of phenomenological time on cosmological time" (Ricoeur, 1983, vol. 3, p. 109).

What appears to be a simple suggestion bears important consequences in the study of narrating in organizations, where subjects cope daily with a temporality that is often conflicting with their personal one and where the role of narrative can be subject to different endings for the subjects involved.


## 1.3   In-betweenness

Furthermore, it is important for me to highlight that narratives live within a dialogic relationship between both mediated and disruptive forms to which they are oriented.

My study on the contextual and relational aspects of both narrating and deciding will search not only for plotted narratives but also for the act of narrating in which the story is not yet there or is challenged or searched for by the narrator. I will also try to explore what the relations are between the dominant stories or narratives and the contingent and local meanings of those stories for the actors involved. Some scholars have used Bakhtin's suggestion of centripetal and centrifugal forces, where centripetal refers to official language and ideology and where centrifugal refers to local and unofficial language. While "the epic world is an utterly finished thing...it is impossible to change, to re-think, to re-evaluate anything in it. It is completed, conclusive and immutable, as a fact, an idea and a value" (Bakhtin, 1981, p. 17). On the contrary the dialogized novel performs the destruction of epic distance and sets its first step in the "comic familiarization of the image of man" (p. 35).

As in the trilogy of movies from Robert Altman *Nashville* (1975), *Short Cuts* (1993) and *Prairie Home Companion* (2006) organizations cannot be exhausted in a single and fixed plot nor in a net of plots, as the essence of a world can never be captured in such simplistic forms. Connections are not only unlimited but also intimate and unpredictable.

In this work I will talk about the everydayness of organizational life. I will argue that people in organizations live in between the plotted and polished narratives and their often compliant, sometimes disruptive storytelling fragments. I will argue that negotiation goes on in every moment of the organizational life of people working in organizations. It is important to notice that it is the in-betweenness, which is always and already there that constitutes everydayness.

In Chapter 7 I will use Bakhtin's concept of dialogic relationship and I–we experience (Bakhtin and Volosinov, 1973) together with Ricoeur's insights on sameness and selfhood (1992), to articulate my findings. The idea is that in-betweenness is always at play at different levels in organizational lives; at work we are in between objects, symbols, rules and discourses to which we are engaged in a dialogic relationship. In-betweenness thus relates, in this context, not only to the social practice of storytelling between individuals but also to the dialogic relations between the subjects and their context and to the infinite combinations in social interactions such as those of organizational life.

Particularly important for this articulation will be the concept of "antenarrative" suggested by Boje (2001). Boje is a management scholar who has devoted most of his career to the study of stories trespassing on the linguistic realm. For this reason it is more than appropriate to cite Boje in this chapter since his insights on narratological terms such as story/narrative definition and his formulation of the notion of antenarrative place him among the most refined storytelling interpreters.

Antenarrative for Boje holds a double meaning "as being before and as a bet...story is an 'ante' state of affairs existing previously to narrative; it is in advance of narrative...secondly, ante is a bet, something to do with gambling and speculation...antenarrative is never final; it is improper" (Boje, 2001, pp. 1–2) and again "stories are 'antenarrative' when told without the proper plot sequence and mediated coherence preferred in narrative theory. These are stories that are too unconstructed and fragmented to be captured by retrospective sense-making" (Boje, 2001, p. 3).

Antenarrative is deeply connected with experience "antenarrative gives attention to the speculative, the ambiguity of sense-making and guessing as to what is happening in the flow of experience" (Boje, 2001, p. 3).

The concept of antenarrative will be of paramount importance in the research performed among the bankers, a particular sensitivity will be devoted to the study of storytelling excerpts where "people are still chasing stories and many different logics for plotting" (Boje, 2001, p. 4).


## 1.4   An alternative mode of knowing

Narrative, along with human time, has to do with the contingent and local meaning of events (Jedlowski, 2000, p. 9).

When I hear the expression "In Lugano it rains 70 days a year" (I am making this up), and supposing that this expression is supported by scientific and proven knowledge, this expression does not say anything about whether or not I should take an umbrella with me on any particular morning. It is only through observation of specific cues pointing to the fact that it is one of those 70 days and my personal attitude toward rain that I can decide whether or not to take my umbrella with me. Looking at the streets we can notice that on rainy days some people carry umbrellas while others do not.

Many scholars have insisted on the differences between scientific and narrative discourse and once again I would like to override such dichotomy, but let me just mention some of these discourses, as they are extremely relevant for narrative epistemology. "Scientific knowledge does not represent the totality of knowledge; it has always existed in addition to, and in competition and conflict with, another kind of knowledge, which I will call narrative in the interest of simplicity" (Lyotard, 1979, p. 7). Similar epistemological foundations are present in narrative discourse as proposed by other scholars (Bruner, 1986; Lyotard, 1979; MacIntyre, 1984) who argued for relative and contextual discourse as the basis of narrative. If scientific discourse relates to truth and universality narrative discourse relates to contingency and the relevant criteria are different from truth, they can be assimilated to justice and/or happiness as in Austin's performatives (Austin, 1962), ethical wisdom, beauty (auditory or visual sensibility), and so on. The result for Lyotard (1979, p. 18) is that it is therefore impossible to judge the existence or validity of narrative knowledge on the basis of scientific knowledge or vice versa. Bruner uses a similar argument "the imaginative application of the paradigmatic (logico-scientific) mode leads to good theory, tight analysis, logical proof, sound argument and empirical discovery guided by reasoned hypothesis... the imaginative use of the narrative mode leads instead to good stories, gripping drama, believable (though not necessarily 'true') historical accounts" (Bruner, 1986, p. 13).

I would add that narrative research allows us to engage with reality on a different level. Since we have argued in the last section that narrative is naturally present in in-betweenness, narrative research can be an open door to the study of subjectivity and to the manifold connections that the individuals hold with their world.

As Marquard puts it "the truth is one thing, but the way we can live with the truth is another. Knowledge serves the former, cognitively and stories serve the latter, vitally... their task (stories) is not to find the truth, but to find a *modus vivendi* with truth" (Marquard, 1989, p. 90).

The suggestion of narration is in its contingency, and it is probably for this reason that we cannot avoid its fascination. It is probably because our lives are not made of universal statements but rather of specific and local meanings, that on the rare occasions that we realize them or we get close to realizing other people's, we feel pervaded by a feeling of belonging to the world. It is the case of the epiphany of Gabriel in Joyce's short story *The Dead* when he hears the story of his wife Gretta and the boy who died in the rain for her.

If stories have little to do with rational explanations of the world they have a lot to do with the intimate experience of the world. I will often refer to this intimate experience of the word where intimacy is a difficult concept to articulate as it tends to escape every classification. It seems to me that the excess between the signifier and the signified in stories is tied to such intimate experience of the world.

## 1.5   Narrating logos or mythos?

Just a last digression on the contingent character of narrative, which is to say the absence of logical necessity of narrative, the fact of being so without having to be so, which brings us back to the bespoken antinomy between *logos* and *mythos* born in the Hellenic philosophical tradition and then developed during enlightenment. These two terms (initially both meaning "word") will assume the expression of the boundary between the rational discourse, the reason, and the word without foundations (in the enlightenment's perspective), something similar to the contemporary terms "rumor" and "gossip".

If, as a result mythos holds a subaltern position compared to logos, this is not the case for Plato who considers mythos as a way to approach logos, and in fact a number of philosophical problems have been explained exactly using the mythos.

A second aspect is that of the development of western culture around the idea of logos as an expression of progress and modernity, while mythos would adapt to backward and uncritical societies.

Even this conception holds a degree of ambivalence as, in our society, traditional and modern elements coexist (according to an idea of selective modernity).

A last consideration, deals with a notion of mythos that reminds us of spontaneous creativity as opposed to the strict rules of argumentation, it is the world of fantasy and dreaming as opposed to conscious thought (psychoanalysis). In this case mythos would connect the self to its most intimate experience of the world. It is the territory of words, not only words that connect (the term logos comes from the root *leg* which evokes the idea of gathering and connecting) but the words that are tied to the emotional sphere, that find meanings that are often precluded to the interpretative schema of reason.

Good narrators know this and narrate accordingly. It is the ludic function of narrative, the enchantment dimension that Jedlowski talks about (Jedlowski, 2000, p. 162).

It is in this very distinction between logos and mythos, and in its innumerable encounters that the postmodern intuition resides, that is to say in the possibility of seeing different systems of sense which are not mutually exclusive, but rather contribute through their incessant construction and deconstruction to experience.

To accept the challenge of complexity (which is also the title of a seminal collection edited by Gianluca Bocchi and Mauro Ceruti, 1985) represents in my view the idea of accepting varied and nonhomogeneous models of rationality, which can be assimilated only through the specificity of the contexts in which they are performed.

Embracing the postmodern attitude, for me, means to accept such a fragmentation of paradigms but yet as Vattimo suggests being content to continue "living in the errant in the light of a fundamentally different attitude" (Vattimo, 1998, p. 171).

I strongly believe that part of this happiness may depend on the stories that we are able to perform or rather on the negotiation going on between plotted narratives and experience at both an individual and relational level.

However, I don't want to open up here what will be developed further in the book and which constitutes an inevitable reference to epistemological considerations whose political and social underpinnings are often source of irreconcilable dogmatisms. It is for this reason that I adopt a pragmatic approach by looking at narratives as practices that are present in our everyday lives in organizations.

## 1.6   Plot: The organization?

When talking about the definition of narrative/discourse/story it is impossible not to mention the notion of plot (present sometime as a synonym of narrative/discourse/*syzhet*), which can be defined according to Brooks (1984) as the organization and presentation of the narrative. Without the plot that organizes it would not be possible to bring together apparently distant and noncontinuous elements into the coherence of a story.

"Plot is first of all, a constant of all written and oral narrative, in that a narrative without at least a minimal plot would be incomprehensible. Plot is the principle of interconnectedness and intention which we cannot do without in moving through the discrete elements – incidents, episodes, actions – of a narrative: even such loosely articulated forms as the picaresque novel display device of interconnectedness, structural repetitions that allow us to construct a whole; and we can make sense of such dense and seemingly chaotic texts as dreams because we use interpretive categories that enable us to reconstruct intentions and connections, to replot the dream as narrative" (Brooks, 1984, p. 5).

Of course the notion of plot has to do with both the notion of *fabula* and *syzhet* and if the temptation is that of arguing that the plot is what organizes the *fabula* into a *syzhet*, we have to be careful not to fall into this simplification. There is a tendency to consider the plot as a way of reconciling often distant and non-coherent elements. This tendency is very important in the study of narratives in organizational life as it accommodates what is the contemporary obsession of sense. And it is for this reason that I think it is important to take some consideration on the matter. If we look up "plot" in the Oxford English Dictionary, and as suggested by Brooks himself, there are at least four meanings of the term, the first refers to a secret plan to do something illegal and harmful; the second refers to the act of devising and presenting the events in a play, novel or a film; the third refers to the marking of a territory; and the fourth regards the relation between two variables in a diagram. The Italian *trama* and the French *trame*, together with the first and the second meaning of the English also refer to texture and weaving, as *trama/trame* is the weft that is passed over and under the warp to make a cloth: it is a fascinating metaphor if we think about the fact that the different colors and threads can become fully visible and enjoyable through the relationship with the warp.

Referring to the second meaning, which is the narratological meaning, there is an idea of devising which itself refers to both an idea of separating, which preludes organization, and to an idea of device in its early sense of will and desire.

It is not surprising then that Brooks insists, throughout his whole book, on the idea of desire in/of the text, talking about power, drive, "becoming energy" (citing Derrida, *entelechia*) and thus providing us with a dynamic concept of plot. Through the plot the subject is able to give a shape to the chaos and to appease his orectic aspiration to order.

Where is Brooks taking us in this discourse and how does this relate to what we have said in the previous paragraphs?

There is no doubt in the fact that sense is produced and reproduced through what Gadamer (1975, p. 261) refers to as "anticipation of completion" capable of organizing experience in a coherent manner.

I will not argue against what is thought to be one of the most common human activities, sense making and that narratives can represent ex-post reconstruction, nor the fact that there is a human strive toward coherence and order especially in our world of uncertainty (or presumed and human made uncertainty). Is doing research that is highly relevant the way to achieve such a sense? Using the words of Lukács, we are far from the man of the world of Epos, an intelligible and finalized world in which the alien reaction to sense is a result only of the distance from it (Lukács, 1920, p. 60). I will not cite here all the authors that have witnessed the shattering of the solidity and the coherence of sense in the philosophical perspective of the last decades. I would just notice how in a context of shattering and loosing of the uniqueness of sense, a discourse on narratives and plot acquires a great importance and why narrative interpretative tools are used more and more in the various domains.

One open question remains: what are the plots that are possible in our world? Brooks himself insists on the relationship between possible plots and the cultural and philosophical reflections that go hand-in-hand with them and which are specific to a particular historical time. In the nineteenth century there is the detective novel – the solution represents the rational explanation, which is able to unveil the most dark and frightening aspects of life. On the contrary the twentieth century novel performs an insolubility of the plot – confronting the reader with comprehension options often contrasting. The plot becomes in this way, according to the Italian and French acceptation and citing Barthes notion, a "texture" of multiple languages, codes that the reader organizes in always different fashions, as in Eco's book *The Name of the Rose* where the levels of interpretations are manifold or in Calvino's *If on a Winter Night a Traveler* where the reader is actually confronted with and reads about how he or she reads the story of the reader who is read. So the novel becomes literature and metaphor of literature at the same time. In what is considered an example of the postmodern novel, Eco offers the humorous and also the melancholic side of experience, when Guglielmo da Baskerville, after chasing order and truth, finally reaches his goal (in the body of the *Poetics* by Aristotle!) he is disappointed because he understands that he used a wrong motive. We can thus only laugh at truth and liberate ourselves from the obsession of truth because the only truths that we need, Eco suggests, are the ones to throw away.

However, sometimes it is hard to live lives (or to perceive them) to the script, according to the "dramatic effect arising from the scene" that Goffman talks about (Goffman, 1959, p. 285). What emerges from the distinctions proposed above is the fact that if we accept that the narrative is a form of action itself, then it becomes difficult to reduce it to simplifying categories. A heavy burden to the reaching of new comprehensions, but moreover a negative thrust to the ability of going beyond the known structures of action. It is often in the ability to agilely configure new plots that our survival is challenged.

When talking about plot and narratives one question that arises is: what exists outside the plot? Are there instances that cannot be reconciled into this organizer? I will come back to this point in the Chapter 7 where I will talk about consolidated narratives that are socially organized and fragments that cannot fit into the organized narrative.

## 1.7   Narrating as a relational and contextual practice

Leaving the distinction between story/discourse and following Genette's indications we get to the third instance of his conception "*narration* = narrating", which unlike *histoire* (whole of events) or *récit* (discourse that refers to such events) concentrates on the act of narrating (Genette, 1972, p. 26).

Such definition is particularly interesting for social sciences as it opens the path to the study of narrative as a practice.

Rather than texts or content, narratives are seen as social practices performed by individuals. Barbara Herrnstein Smith proposes a definition of narrative as "someone tells someone else that something happened" (Herrnstein Smith, 1981, p. 228). She thus relaxes the assumption of two connected events and the beginning, middle, end as the minimum condition for narrativity. She also argues that "a related advantage of conceiving narrative this way – which is to say as a part of a social transaction – is that it encourages us to notice and explore certain aspect of narratives that tend to remain obscure or elusive when we conceive of it primarily as kind of text or structure or any other detached and decontextualized entity … every telling is produced and experienced under certain social conditions and constraints and that it always involves two parties, an audience as well as a narrator … and yet … the nature of the interests involved on both sides may vary greatly from one transaction to another" depending on "the particular social and circumstantial conditions that elicit and constrain the behavior of each of them". Narratives are "acts, the features of which – like features of all other acts – are functions of the variable sets of conditions in response to which they are performed" (Herrnstein Smith, 1981, pp. 228–229).

Herrnstein Smith's definition provides a wider field for narrative including not only texts but also oral accounts. Talking about the relation to the listener we can distinguish between written and oral storytelling (conversational storytelling will be the focus of my research), noticing that in the form of written text, the relationship between the author and the reader is a distant one, and no response is possible from the reader. This is not true for oral forms of storytelling where a listener or an audience is present. Every story has an audience; the relationship between the narrator and the audience influences the narration in the same way as content and form of narration influence the relationship. Also the functions of narration (that I will expose in the second chapter) change according to the relation in which they are inscribed.

Genette's third instance *narration* refers to the social practice of narrating, which is eluded by narratologist's interest. The focus of narratoligists is in between Genette's acceptation of *histoire* and *récit*. If we study the teller and the listener we are outside narratologists' interests.

What we have to understand is that when narratologists talk about teller and listener they are talking about internal instances within the texts, they are not talking about real people, real narrators.

In any case, argumentations in favor of narrative as practices performed by tellers in relation to a listener and organized for specific purposes seem to fit the complex environments in which organizational discourses are performed.

It is the approach of narration conceived as a communicative and thus social practice that opens the way to the use of the studies of pragmatics rather than philosophy of language, sociology or anthropology for the actualization in an organizational context.

When we talk about the act of narrating we get very close to the concept of utterance, that is to say a communicative exchange between two interlocutors. Using again the words of Bakhtin "the expression utterance is determined by the actual conditions of the given utterance – above all by its immediate social situation ... the word is oriented toward an addressee ... and in the absence of the real addressee, an addressee is presupposed" (Bakhtin and Volosinov, 1973, p. 85). From this apparently simple recipe Bakhtin derives a relational and social orientation of the utterance. He situates it at every broader social milieu level: scientific, philosophic as well as in everyday life and at work (Bakhtin and Volosinov, 1973).

The French linguist Benveniste has worked to a theory of utterance, as has in a different approach the philosopher of language Austin, with his bespoken book *How do to things with words*. It is very interesting to notice that the work of the two, albeit toward very different orientations seem to be complementary.[3] As a matter of fact while the first affirms that the context influences utterance the second affirms that the utterance can influence the context. We may go even further to considerate that utterances constitute the context but I don't wish to enter here into speech theory. What I would certainly retain is the idea of narrating practices and their inclusion in a theory of speech acts and action, which considers the social and relational aspects of both. The social orientation of communication is very present in my work. As Bakhtin argues, we always address somebody (even if not present) who in return is always present in the sense of construction of the utterance on the same level as the other social elements of the contexts of expression. Expression cannot be understood outside the context in which it is performed and to what it is in relation with. "Orientation of the word toward the addressee has an extremely high significance. In point of fact, word is a two-sided act. It is determined equally by whose word it is and for whom it is meant. As a word, it is precisely the product of the reciprocal relationship between speaker and listener, addresser and addressee. Each and every word expresses the "one in relation to the other…the immediate social situation and the broader social milieu wholly determine – and determine from within, so to speak – the structure of an utterance" (Bakhtin and Volosinov, 1973, p. 86). But of course personal experience is not irrelevant, and the process is not transparent. Bakhtin continues: "a distinction can be made between two poles, two extremes between which an experience can be apprehended and ideologically structured, tending now toward the one, now toward the other". Let us label these two extremes the "I-experience" and the "we-experience". In the I-experience the more "it approaches its extreme limit, the more it loses its ideological structuredness and…also loses its verbal delineation". The "we-experience is differentiated…allows of different degrees and different types of ideological structuring" (Bakhtin and Volosinov, 1973, pp. 87–88). Some very important implications are drawn: first is that the individual utterance (*parole*) is never an individual fact and as expressed by Bakhtin itself "the actual reality of language speech is not the abstract system of linguistic forms, not the isolated monologic utterance, and not the psycho-physiological act of its implementation, but the social event of verbal interaction implemented in a utterance or utterances" (p. 94); and yet "verbal communication can never be understood and explained outside of this connection with a concrete situation" (p. 95). The utterance always needs a context, while proposition does not. The social aspect of the utterance is double: the utterance is always addressed to somebody (even if not present, as in "generalized other", Mead, 1934) and the teller is a social being him or herself. As elaborated by Watzlawick, Beavin, Jackson (1967) and Bateson (1972), we can affirm not only that we always talk to somebody but also that we are already in a social relationship with the world even before talking. It is the pragmatic level of communication. It is not difficult to comprehend this as we have all been faced at least once with a situation in which we can't for instance catch the humor. We follow the semantic and syntactic level but this doesn't give us any cue. And this also leads us to the conclusion that meaning holds a degree of ambiguity which only context can dissolve. But context is not always transparent and nonambiguous, and individuals experience it in unlimited ways.

It is important here to stress the social and relational constituency character of oral narrative practices from a communicational and sociological point of view.

Genette introduces with the act of narrating, the narrator, the storyteller, the "who" of the stories, often shading in both *histoire* and *récit*. My study of the Southwestern Bank is a study of narrational practices and a study of narrators, in the context of an evolution/transformation of organizational life. For this reason the sensitivity of the research is closer to Benjamin's *Storyteller* (1936), than that of narratology scholars. The work of Paolo Jedlwoski and his sociological understanding of narrative practices in everyday life have informed my research. Jedlowski's work is inscribed in a sociological tradition of studies of everyday life in Italy (Jedlowski and Leccardi, 2003), which is particularly sensitive to the importance of storytelling practices in everyday social relations.[4]

# 2
# Narrative Research in Organizational Studies

The first part of this chapter provides an overview of the encounter between organizational studies and narrative research through the work of the scholars that have made this possible.

Such an encounter is not the result of a single contact at a specific time but rather a long process of reconsideration of taken for granted beliefs in the social sciences that has led to the possibility of the legitimating of narrative research. Some of these aspects have been already pointed out in Chapter 1, where the different definitions of narrative, story and storytelling were outlined. Such definitions go in fact hand in hand with the epistemological foundations that have supported them.

In the second part of the chapter I will provide examples of narrative research in organizational studies and in particular in studies of decision-making. This chapter will serve as a bridge from the first part of the book to the second part of the book where all of these concepts will be applied to a specific case: that of a small community bank being acquired by a large corporate bank in the south of New Mexico.

In both the second and third part of the work I will be constantly confronted with the theoretical foundations that have made the narrative research possible as they represent both a methodological framework and a key to interpretation. It is interesting to notice that narrative research's appeal actually lies in the process of doing research and engaging with reality rather than in normative assumptions.

## 2.1  Communication as an event

One of the major influences in narrative research has been the shift from the view of communication and language as simple tools to represent reality to a view of language as a constituent of reality. Language and communication in management studies were for long time considered and studied as mere tools, and "typically presented as a pragmatic problem related to the managerialist concerns of organizational effectiveness and management practice. The concern was with the problems of communication structures, patterns and practices and their impact on the efficacy of the managerial task and the effective operation of organization systems. Language was viewed naively and simply as the medium of communication, its ontological status was not at issue, its epistemological role unexplored" (Westwood and Linstead, 2001). The main concern was then how managers could communicate better inside and outside their organizations in order to achieve effectiveness and reputation. This is still on the agenda of many communication studies in the management realm.

Management studies and organizational studies were probably among the last ones in the social sciences to be touched by what is known as "linguistic turn" or "linguistic shift". Such a turn is a body of thought characterized by the focusing on language as an active constituent of reality rather than just a tool to report on it. Rorty, in *The Linguistic Turn*, discussed this for the first time. *Essays in Philosophical Method* in 1967 (Rorty, 1967) was the one that actually coined the expression "linguistic turn" to refer to the contribution of linguistic philosophy the idea that philosophical problems can be solved either through language or through a better understanding of it.

As Crespi indicated in *Sociologia del Linguaggio* (2005), different theoretical and cultural components have contributed to this turn: the analytical philosophy of language and hermeneutical philosophy along with the evolution of structuralist linguistics (Crespi, 2005, p. 43). The point of convergence is the idea of language "in action", as an active constituent of reality.

Different authors see the *Philosophical Investigations* of Wittgenstein as the starting point of this understanding. Wittgenstein's work is in this sense pioneering as he placed the role of language in relation to reality at the center of his life-long research, reaching some of the most refined interpretations of the phenomena. In his later work (Wittgenstein, 1958) he argues that the meaning of words cannot be understood outside the particular context in which they are used: as in a game the move can be understood only in reference to previous moves and to the particular game played. In other words meaning cannot be found in the word itself or in any pure activity of the mind, and this is the major revolution of what is called the linguistic turn.

The seminal contribution of Wittgenstein's work stands in the conception that reality and language are not separate entities, as the meanings of our thoughts and expression do not exist outside language itself. To me the interest in the linguistic turn for narrative research is in the idea that language is in action, is situated in a context, where context though is not a nonambiguous entity that can easily lead to meaning, but is rather interpreted at every moment and every level. Meaning would thus depend on the definition of context that we are able to attribute.

The famous example Bakhtin employs is that of the two people sitting silent in a room: "Then one of them says, 'Well!' The other does not respond" (Bakhtin and Volosinov, 1976, p. 99); later on we apprehend that both interlocutors were looking at the window and since it was still snowing and it was May they are both disappointed by the late snowfall. All this is assumed in the simple word "Well!".

The utterance for Bakhtin is lively, is active, solves a situation, it does not merely reflect a situation: it is a situation. That in return influences other situations and other utterances. Meaning can thus be caught only in an endless chain of signifiers and with reference to infinitive other communicative acts.

Narratives in the same way are events that are related to reality or toward a representation of it, but also constitute a new reality. Of course this is not a property of narrative or language but rather a way to engage in research on it, this is why in the next section I will talk about the role of the researcher and the researched and the novelty of the narrative paradigm in this sense.

## 2.2   The role of the researcher and the researched

This section follows some considerations developed in the first chapter regarding the existence of a preexisting and independent reality and the role of narration.

Following the solution proposed, narrative inquiry finds its specificity exactly in this relationship. Narration is shaped by experience and shapes experience; although it exists independently of the researcher, once it is studied it cannot be considered independently by the act of studying. Experience is the "fundamental ontological category" of narrative research, argues Clandinin (2006, p. 38). Clandinin proposes, drawing from Dewey, a pragmatist approach of experience that seems well suited for narrative research. "Empirical method will present inquiry as a series of choices, inspired by purposes that are shaped by past experience, undertaken through time, and will trace the consequences of these choices in the whole of an individual or community's lived experience" (Clandinin, 2006, p. 39). I will come back to these arguments in the fourth chapter where I will describe the methodology used in my empirical research.

I think it is important here, though, to point out that the relationship between the researcher and the researched is central to contemporary sociology. As Melucci pointed out, we passed from the dichotomy observer/field to the idea of the observer-in-the-field who is placed in social relations and in relation to the observed field (Melucci, 1998, pp. 22–23). The idea is the researcher is not a neutral medium in research but constitutes part of the research itself. The type of research I have conducted does not neglect this role but is actually based on the familiarization between the interviewer and the interviewee. As I will explain in the fourth chapter, the result I obtained in terms of richness of the interviews would have not be possible without an involvement in the field that required weekly visits to the bankers at different premises and the building of trust and familiarity.

As argued in chapter one the relational aspect of storytelling is paramount. For this reason and, as it will be said in the fourth chapter, the way interviewee interprets interviewer will influence the amount and the orientation of the stories.

## 2.3  Studying stories

Telling stories is part of our everyday life, people tell stories to other people in different social intercourses. If some part of research is interested in strong generalizations of systematic cause effect relations between abstract objects, narrative inquiry is an exploration into human ordinary unpredictable interaction.

Away from the desire of creating "grand theories" narrative researchers seek the particular, embedded in a context that can never be neglected. It is a kind of research that tends to overcome the classical dichotomy between structure and agency typical of the European sociological tradition (which is less relevant in the United States where it is referred to as "macro" and "micro" aspects) and rejects the dogmatism of both societal determinacy and individual indeterminacy as explanatory paradigms.

Everyday life and storytelling practices represent rather a continuous tension between what Jedlowski (1994) refers to as "common sense" and "experience". Common sense is both socialized and historicized, while experience has to do with the subjectivity that makes it relevant and novel at the same time. I will show how storytelling acts constitute a privileged lens when talking about practices. The storytelling act witnesses the constant movement between two poles: the stabilizing forms of social determinacy and the destabilizing forms of experience.

Here is the dilemma: on the one hand determinacy is an indispensable device for social acknowledgment and it orients and structures social practices, but, on the other hand its reductionist character cannot fit with the complexity of experience and its uniqueness.

Ricoeur (1992) has used the concepts of sameness (*idem*) and selfhood (*ipse*) to describe two modes of permanence to which narrative performs the role of mediator between "the pole of character, where *idem* and *ipse* tend to coincide, and the pole of self-maintenance, where selfhood frees itself from sameness" (p. 199). "Narrative identity oscillate between two limits: a lower limit, where permanence in time expresses the confusion of *idem* and *ipse*; and an upper limit, where the *ipse* poses the question of its identity without the aid and support of the *idem*" (p. 124).

In the seventh chapter where I will come back to these arguments I will also use the concept of antenarrative described by Boje (2001). Antenarrative is before narrative, is before the order and structure of retrospective interpretation. Antenarrative is in the flow of experience.

However, this is a further step that I will articulate more clearly in the third part of the book. It is important to point out here that the sociological concept of practice, whose articulation can be retraced to Bourdieu (1990) and Giddens (1984), can be perfectly fitting for the narrative lenses. As a matter of fact studying organizational practices means studying organization at a contextual level rather than an objectified level. Organizational phenomena are in this sense constructed within organization in social interactions (Gherardi, 2005). Studying practices displays an enormous potential for communication research as well, since the social construction of reality is linguistically achieved. It is for this reason that some authors, such as Jedlowski (2007) use the term "narrative practice" instead of "narrative action".

## 2.4 Narrative inquiry in organizational research: an overview

Narrative inquiry in organizational research starts in the seventies with the two studies that are considered the first studies in narrative research in management: one is Clark's study of three American colleges (1972) and the other is the study by Mitroff and Kilmann (1975). In the first study Clark describes the organizational saga of each of the three colleges and argues that although they differ they hold the same function for self-management. Similarly Mitroff and Kilmann argue, even in their title, that the stories managers tell are a new tool for organizational problem solving. Narrative research is thus quite young research in organizational studies but it has nonetheless acquired a considerable status in the organizational sciences and has proved an extensive body of work (Boje, 1991, 2001; Czarniawska, 1997b, 2004; Czarniawska and Gagliardi, 2003; Gabriel, 2004).

It is not a unitary body of work as the levels of analysis and often the purposes of researches are quite different. For this reason it is very difficult to give justice to the complex body of work done in the last 15 years in the field. I will therefore concentrate on what are common features of narrative works and what are, on the other hand, points of divergence.

Following a distinction proposed by Barbara Czarniawska (1997a) narrative has entered the organizational domain in at least three forms: the first is that of people telling stories within organizations; the second is that of seeing organizational life and organizational phenomena as a form of narrative; and the third is that of organizational research as a form of narrative itself.

I will not focus here on the second and third level of interpretation, as the subject of my research is not that of a meta-discourse on organizational studies. I will rather use the acceptation of storytelling organizations that includes both the stories collected among the people belonging to organizations and the stories the organization tells about itself.

Following Czarniawska's acceptation and the storytelling organization acceptation, the first level is that of the researcher who collects stories in the forms of anecdotes, gossip, rumors, myths and so on. They can be spontaneously told or evoked during interviews by the researcher.

In 1991, Boje published a bespoke article on storytelling in organizations (Boje, 1991) that was the result of participant observation in a large office supply firm. Boje collected spontaneous storytelling in various "social scenes" which "included executive meetings held on- and off-site: in conference rooms, restaurants, sales training sessions, as well as conversations in hallways and automobiles" (p. 110).

In the next section I will go into the details of Boje's 1991 findings. For a general overview we can say that his work is inscribed in the effort of giving justice to the relational storytelling practices always going on in organizations. Boje has studied stories has they happen in conversation, drawing from the work of Harvey Sacks, and has focused on the role of the listener as coproducer.

> As listeners, we are co-producers with the teller of the story performance. It is an embedded and fragmented process in which we fill in the blanks and gaps between the lines with our own experience in response to cues, like "You know the story!" Because of what is not said, and yet shared, the audible story is only a fraction of the connection between people in their co-production performance. We become even more of a co-producer when we begin to prompt the teller with cues, such as head nods, changes in posture, and utterances that direct the inquiry (i.e. "One version I heard....";
> "Then, what happened?") and respond with our own data. The story can be conceptualized as a joint performance of teller(s) and hearer(s) in which often overlooked, very subtle utterances play an important role in the negotiation of meaning and co-production in a storytelling episode.
>
> (p. 107)

As we can see this kind of inquiry is very close to the acceptation of narration as a social practice discussed in the first chapter.

Yannis Gabriel, in the same year, collected spontaneous stories: "grassroots stories, generated spontaneously, and disseminated by the word of mouth" (Gabriel, 1991, p. 872) in different work and military organizations. He found three organizational stories that "were part of the local core rather than official organizational cultures" (p. 872). Gabriel argues that:

> ...stories, gossip, myths and jokes may represent attempt to humanize the impersonal spaces of bureaucratic organizations, to mark them as human territory in a similar way to the vase of flowers or the family picture on the executive desk...Many organizations, like the three which provided the context for these stories, are not generally pleasant places in which to live or work. They place severe restrictions on the individual's rights and freedoms and allow little room for those aspects of the human soul which are not directly relevant to the organizational objectives.
>
> (p. 873)

Stories represent for Gabriel "symbolic means of coping with pain" as the three stories told in the organizational contexts studies "they did a lot to sooth, to console, to reconcile" (p. 873).

There are many different ways of collecting stories as well as many objects of study, in some cases stories have been collected in order to understand organizational aspects such as identity, culture, organizational change and learning, just to name few. For example Orr (1990, 1996) collected stories of copy machines employees, and discovered the crucial role of storytelling in problem solving. I will talk about this study in the section devoted to narrative and decision-making at the end of the chapter.

The levels of analysis that Czarniawska talks about are not of course mutually exclusive and in my empirical research I will show how stories collected at the first level cannot neglect influences for considerations on the other levels.

The researcher chooses the first level of analysis, focussing on narrative as social and relational practices, while, in my view, the second or third level (which are quite similar in their endeavor) can refer to two different research paths. On the one side they may relate to an acceptation of narrative closer to that of a text and thus can be subjected to formalist endeavors, while on the other they can be used in a critical acceptation as a text to deconstruct.

The one proposed by Barbara Czarniawska is just a possible frame for revising the work done in the field, but even within this classification there are many differences between the researches. This is true, because far from being defined in a common way; narratives have been studied according to the specificity of the different epistemological traditions and the sensitivity of the scholars that have worked in the field.

Already in the first chapter we have seen how the definition of story and narrative changes across different epistemological areas. Formalists' definitions differ from socio-constructionists' definitions or post-structuralists' definitions and so on. The narrative research done in organizational contexts is not immune from such influences. Almost every author in the organizational domain has interpreted narrative research and declined it in different and unique ways. It is not uncommon that the same author has over time changed or shaped his or her previous epistemological foundations. Boje's work for example can be assimilated with social constructionism when it comes to his 1991 work on organizational storytelling, while later work can be assimilated with post-structuralist and then critical theory and postmodern thought.

Different paradigms can also coexist in the same work as in the case of Czarniawska's work on the Swedish public sector (1997), which can be assimilated with social constructionism with the use of a structuralist device in the form of Burke's scene-act ratio.

The work I will present in the second part of the book is informed to different degrees by social constructionism, post-structuralism and critical theories. I believe it would be difficult to situate narrative researchers into one rigid paradigm and for this reason I would rather talk about different narrative research paths, where epistemological foundations must be paired with methodological aspects and object of the study.

The last section of this chapter, for example, will be devoted to a specific object of narrative research: that of decision-making. Other objects of study could be organizational culture, organizational identity, gender, power, change and so on.

In an encyclopedic effort of narrative research in the organizational realm I think that at least four dimensions should be considered: epistemological foundations; methodology; object of study and definition of story/narrative. The notion itself of narrative comes into question across different authors, as each of them has provided a different point of view on the subject.

It can be argued that narrative analysis in the management domain has dealt mainly with the idea of narrative (justly used instead of story) as a sense-making device. The power of narratives stands in the legitimation of an alternative paradigm for conceiving order and organization. Narrative is, following this acceptation, a way to make sense, to organize, to know, or a way to understand how sense-making is reproduced in organizations.

As argued in the early Czarniawska's work, "A story consists of a plot comprising causally related episodes that culminate in a solution to a problem" (Czarniawska, 1997b, p. 78); and later, "For them to become a narrative, they require a plot, that is, some way to bring them into a meaningful whole" (Czarniawska, 1999, p. 2).

On the other hand focusing on narrative as a social practice may lead the way to the notion of "good story" (Czarniawska, 2004) and to the social implication of the telling of the story. In this case sense-making is just one way of interpreting the narrating practices. A sociological distinction over the different functions that storytelling can perform has been made by Jedlwoski (2000). The communitarian function refers to the relational dimension of narrating, that is to say the relation between the teller and the listener, narrating is in this sense to share a story, "this function corresponds to what narrative most commonly presupposes and produces: a mutual belonging, a sense of sharing" (Jedlowski, 2000, p. 161). On the other hand, the referential function has to do with the content of what is narrated. Storytelling is a way of sharing the knowledge of certain events. The narrated content can belong to real life or to a fictitious world, what characterizes this kind of function is that the focus is on the content of what it is narrated. Of course when we share the knowledge of certain events it is almost impossible not to also share our emotions and feelings about them. Jedlowski continues by saying that narrative can also have a training function, for example in the case of practical instructions, moral precepts or enlightening anecdotes, and in some cases we can see a striking normative function of narratives: narrative becomes a controlling device or a social integration driver. In this case norms are not expressed in an abstract way but rather embedded in specific and paradigmatic examples. Rumors and gossip can serve this function. In other situations the sense of narration is better captured in the entertainment it produces, it is the ludic function, which recalls the notion of play, of the game dimension. A less explicit function is the cognitive function, which is present when we analyze the story as a way to make sense of reality, a way of connecting events and different elements, as abovementioned with regard to organizational research.

Another functional area is that of the identity function which has to do with the identity of the people involved in narration, in this case to share a story is to "express, to construct, to confirm or to look for, through relation, the recognition of identity" (Jedlowski, 2000, p. 162). Identity can be that of the teller or that of the listener as well, as identity is always relative to both and to share a story is to "construct the existence of a 'we' " (Jedlowski, 2000, p. 163).

In the end the commemorative function of narrating is the one that ties different generations. When we narrate we share a story, we save and transmit a story and in this way we avoid the story being forgotten. Narratives are the materials of collective memory.

However, the idea of functions is questioned by the author in the book, who in the end is not satisfied with such distinctions, as he argues that the idea of function itself is misleading in his view as no narration practice can clearly belong to one or the other function, and yet all the functions cannot unveil the irreducible dimension of human experience.

What emerges from all of the distinctions proposed above is the fact that if we accept that narrative is a form of action in itself it becomes irreducible to simplifying categories.

As Cooper puts it: "Instead of an external world of stable objects that support our needs and purposes, the space and time of daily life begins to look like a restless scene of act in permanent suspension, that never reach a final goal" (Cooper, 2005, p. 1690).

We can argue that narratives can be seen as a model of thinking and studied as sense-making tools, that they are a way of creating cultural belonging and transmitting social practices, that they are vehicles of ideologies and instruments of power, that they are a way to come to terms with the temporality of our existence, that they are entertaining but they are at the same time more than all of this.

## 2.5   Storytelling organization

In this section I will further investigate the research on storytelling organizations through the work of Boje. In particular I will try to outline Boje's research path on storytelling organizations, through his two most acclaimed works.

One of the most cited works of Boje is the 1991 *Administrative Science's* article in which he articulates the concept of "storytelling organization". Boje has collected stories in situ as they naturally occurred:

> Everyday organization conversations were taped to capture spontaneous storytelling episodes among seven executives and twenty-three managers, customers, and vendors of a large office-supply firm ... The data set consists of over 100 hours of tape recordings, along with video-recordings of two corporate-sponsored focus groups with key customers and vendors. Where video or tape recording was not feasible, field notes were used as a supplement.
>
> (Boje, 1991, p. 110)

This work is deeply influenced by social constructionism. Boje claims, "In organizations, storytelling is the preferred sense making currency of human relationships among internal and external stakeholders" (Boje, 1991, p. 106) and that the storytelling organization is a "collective storytelling system in which the performance of stories is a key part of members' sense-making and a means to allow them to supplement individual memories with institutional memory" (Boje, 1991, p. 105).

People in organizations

> engage in a dynamic process of incremental refinement of their stories about new events as well as on-going reinterpretations of culturally sacred storylines. When a decision is at hand, the old stories are recounted and compared to unfolding story lines to keep the organization from repeating historically bad choices and to invite the repetition of past successes. In a turbulent

environment, the organization halls and offices pulsate with a story life of the here and now that is richer and more vibrant that the firm's environments."

(Boje, 1991, p. 106)

Concerning the definition of story/narrative, Boje introduces the idea of story as not having a full plot and a complete character, "people told their stories in bits and pieces, with excessive interruptions of story starts, with people talking over each other to share story fragments, and many aborted storytelling attempts" (Boje, 1991, pp. 112–113), opening the path to the idea of multiple and competing voices, multiple stories and multiple interlocutors.

Also interesting for narrative research is the introduction of the concept of "terse story", which is the storytelling of a particular event that is abbreviated in future accounts and becomes comprehensible only to the people that "know the story". Here is how Boje defines terse storytelling:

But just how abbreviated can a story be and still be classified as a story? The shortest story form is when one person says to the other, "You know the story!" It can be so brief that the performance is barely distinguishable from other non-performance utterances. I call this filling-in the-blanks form terse storytelling. Much of the story that is told is not actually uttered. A terse telling is an abbreviated and succinct simplification of the story in which parts of the plot, some of the characters, and segments of the sequence of events are left to the hearer's imagination.

(Boje, 1991, p. 115)

One terse story in Boje's 1991 research is "the parking sign story" which "concerns how, upon Doug's arrival as the new CEO, a non-gone executive tried to implement reserved parking privileges for executives. Doug, in almost his first meeting with the executives, uprooted a 'reserved for the CEO' (one was also reserved for each of the VPs) parking sign and threw it on the executive meeting table, demanding to know 'who put up this sign? This is not the kind of leadership I will have around here.' The offending executive, for this and other good reasons, was fired by week's end" (Boje, 1991, p. 119).

Boje argues that the way "the teller picks one aspect to abbreviate ('You know the rest of the story') and another to accentuate ('It's the same old story, except this time we found them together')" (Boje, 1991, p. 123) makes it a significant concept for narrative researchers. Also "part of storytelling involves managing the telling of a story by being able to weave it into on-going conversation. Both teller and listener are sending cues to manage how much of the story is told, how much is left to the imagination, and what interpretation is applied" (Boje, 1991, p. 123).

In my study of the bank I find several of these terse stories running through the accounts of the bankers such as Anthony's story, the tower's story and so on. The study of terse storytelling dynamics was part of the research strategy used.

Boje also talks about glosses or glossing:

A story gloss is a brief retelling of a piece of a story so that the referent experience becomes sensible in new ways after having been glossed. The gloss is akin to marginal notes or digression that can exaggerate, simplify, and shift the meaning of the experience. Storytellers might use a gloss as an occasion to accentuate an anomalous experience as an integral aspect of the founding, maturity, reform, or demise of an organization.

(Boje, 1991, p. 116)

As Boje points out:

The most important implication for organization study that was born out of the present study is that story researchers can benefit by entering organizations to observe first-hand how people perform storytelling. The focus in traditional organization story research has been on texts taken from a range of isolated, often anomalous stories plucked out of their natural setting. These studies ignore performance and streamline the stories or treat them as so many variables that can give empirical explanations of the organization. The storytelling organization theory posits story text and performance as two sides of the same coin and gives us insight into the complex and varied ways organization members use storytelling in their work world.

(Boje, 1991, p. 126)

In 1995 Boje published another important article in the *Academy of Management Journal* in which he presented his study of Walt Disney Company.

This article already shows his move into post-structuralism and critical theory as is posits that storytelling organizations cannot be reduced to one "grand narrative" or "grand story" but rather they are a "pluralistic construction of multiplicity of stories, storytellers, and story performance events that are like Tamara but are realized differently depending upon the stories in which one is participating". (Boje, 1995, p. 1000)

Tamara is a play,

> where a dozen characters unfold their stories before a walking, sometimes running, audience... of remaining stationary, viewing a single stage, the audience fragments into small groups that chase characters from one room to the next, from one floor to the next, even going into bedrooms, kitchens, and other chambers to chase and co-create the stories that interest them the most. If there are a dozen stages and a dozen storytellers, the number of story lines an audience could trace as it chases the wandering discourses of Tamara is 12 factorial (479,001,600).
>
> (Boje, 1995, p. 997)

This time the storytelling collected was both spontaneous and official:

> I began collecting Disney stories in 1989 and spent the entire summer of 1990 at the Disney archives, where I recorded all the stories I could find in Disney's ample supply of audio and video tapes... I was allowed to collect examples of Disney leaders engaged in storytelling by using my handheld tape recorder to sample the archival recordings. Initially, I focused upon Disney leaders engaged in storytelling work in speeches, work interactions, documentary interviews, and seemingly impromptu conversations. In addition to a stock of TV shows, films, and cartoon shorts, the archived record contained CEO discourse.
>
> (Boje, 1995, p. 1003)

Boje used deconstruction and postmodern theory to unfold the different premodern, modern and postmodern stories. The analysis suggested "that organizations are not exclusively pre-modern, modern, or postmodern but composed of fragmented, competing discourses" (Boje, 1995, p. 1031) and that "organizational life is more indeterminate, more differentiated, more chaotic, than it is simple, systematic, monological, and hierarchical" (Boje, 1995, p. 1001).

The official and founding stories of Walt and the Magic Kingdom were paired with marginal or excluded stories of strikes, reprimands and Tayloristic practices, showing us the distance that can occur between official and parallel stories performed by organizations. An interesting view on storytelling organizations research is provided by Gabriel (2004) who affirms:

> On the one had we have realized that there are official organizational stories, stories reproduced in organizational rituals, advertisements, websites, and official publications ... these may include narratives of great achievements, of missions successfully accomplished, of crises successfully overcome, of dedicated employees, effective managers and heroic leaders. In addition to such narratives, however, and often in direct opposition to them, we have become aware of a wide range of stories existing outside the managed terrains of organizations ... there are times where such stories build on organizational stories, develop them and qualify them. More often, however, such stories remain stubbornly indifferent to the official stories or alternatively explicitly challenge, ridicule or subvert organizational texts ... such stories express a wide range of emotions including anger, bitterness, pride, hope, nostalgia, fear, anxiety, shame, guilt, happiness and love and capture powerfully some of the diverse experiences of organizational members enabling them to make sense of these experiences, and even to endure them when they are hard or brutalizing.
>
> (Gabriel, 2004, pp. 3–4)

For Gabriel "stories open valuable windows into the emotional, political and symbolic lives of organizations, offering researchers a powerful instrument for carrying out research" and let us "gain access to deeper organizational realities, closely linked to their members' experiences" (Gabriel, 2004, p. 2).

## 2.6   Narratives and decision-making

In this section I will talk about the relationship between narrative and decision-making, which was the original core of the research.

This aspect is no longer the focus of the research but is nevertheless present in the interviews I carried out and I believe it is interesting to see the possible encounters with narrative theory. In particular here I will point out scholars that have studied decision-making and narrative using a sensitivity that is close to mine. I moved myself along the narrative research realm and find myself closer to the sociological interpretation and pragmatic view often times cited in this work.

I won't quote here the work of scholars that argue in favor of the use of stories as a transparent tool to achieve linear change in organization and who have legitimized the entering in the marketplace of a number of story consultants[5].

There is a temptation of arguing that to narrate is to decide and to decide is to narrate, but I will argue that we need to overcome it for a number of reasons. The reasons are all intertwined, if we accept narrative as a sense-making device (which I found quite reductive) we can't infer that from sense-making and choice there is a direct link, and the same can be said if we accept that narrative is a way of knowing, as the link between knowledge and agency is similarly problematic, if we finally accept that narrating and deciding are forms of action the problem of identity becomes even more problematic, should we narrate first and then decide or should we decide and then narrate? But if there is no identity between the two, we can still relate to some forms of possible encounters.

Some have argued that there is a relationship between deciding and narrative, as narrative can serve as guides in decision-making. Narrative serves in this case as frames.

In his study of photocopy technicians, Orr (1990, 1996) argues that narratives can function as guides as workers memorize collective stories of problem solving. Orr describes two photocopy repair technicians from Xerox. When dealing with a photocopy machine that is not functioning and presents error codes that are not exact, they are able to solve their problems telling each other stories about similar situations that they have encountered in the past. Narrating thus helps them in recognizing the situation through the activation of shared stories and becomes a diagnostic frame. The interaction between memories, experiences and intuition will lead to the solution of the problem. The story of this solution will then be told again when playing cards at the factory canteen and will thus become part of the collective memory of the occupational community and will be used again in other contexts.

More generally we can argue that narratives can be related to decision-making as they suggest (or rather have to do with) plots and genres. As in Orr's work technicians "value their job both for the challenge of the work and for the identity as hero. Competent practice at the job creates the identity, and their stories celebrate both the practice and the heroism while preserving the details of the practice and so helping to perpetuate the identity" (Orr, 1996, pp. 160–161).

Stories, and in particular the "war stories" about difficult and unusual cases, have different functions; they represent a way to sort out information in order to determine the diagnosis "the practice of diagnosis is done through narrative, and both diagnosis and process are preserved and circulated among the technicians through war stories, anecdotes of their experiences" (Orr, 1996, p. 104); they perform as strong identitarian function as the telling of these narratives "demonstrates and shares the technicians' mastery and so both celebrates and creates the technicians' identities as master of the black arts of dealing with machines…"(Orr, 1996, p. 2).

This experience, which passes on from mouth to mouth revitalizes Benjamin's traditional storytelling in the orientation toward practical interests. "…every real story. It contains, openly or covertly, something useful. The usefulness may, in one case, consist in a moral; in another, in some practical advice; in a third, in a proverb or maxim" (Benjamin, 1936). This function has not disappeared in organizational context as Orr's impressive work demonstrates.

Getting back to organizational decision-making, one of the most powerful suggestions, and unfortunately one of very few in the field, is given by O'Connor (1996) "we may view organizational decision-making as a convergence of narratives that are in Heidegger's distinctive phrase 'always already' going on". She demonstrates how executives produce narratives about themselves and their organizations before a decision is made and how decision blends these narratives together.

Secondly, she shows how decisions are human constructs and not "natural phenomena in the world that we discover, they are made by theorists, observers and participants. As the etymology of the word decision suggests, when we mark something as a decision, we set it off from its background in a particular way – we cut it out of a larger narrative or of other narratives" and argue for a narrative form of the garbage can decision process saying that "narratives that define choice opportunities, problems and solutions as such converge with the always already occurring narratives of decision makers. And decision theory (i.e., narrative about these narratives) converges with the always already occurring narratives of decision theorists" (O'Connor, 1996, p. 318).

Decisions have to do more with "incisions" or "the ontological act of cutting and partitioning off a version of reality from was has hitherto been indistinguishable" (Cooper, 1986) than with intentionality, consequentiality and optimization. It is in this context that narrating as a social practice becomes relevant, in a view of organizations envisioned not only as "commercial and administrative structures directed by specific goals" but also as "strategies for ordering disorder, for making sense out of the senseless and for providing a language of images and mental maps for dealing with the meaningless infinity that Weber saw as a prime motivator in human society" (Cooper, 2001, p. 328). I believe that narrating has to do with order and identity as much as with the "rude, untamed and excessive energies that lie beneath the rational glosses" (Cooper, 2001, p. 323).

Decision-making will be, in my research, treated as part of the executive work, part of executive work's experience and identity. If we consider work as socially constructed through language, we can legitimize the study of decision-making in an organizational context by collecting organizational storytelling about organizational decisions. On the one hand storytelling can represent a guide, a repertoire, as in Orr's problem solving case, or can function as an ex post legitimating tool, as O'Connor seems to suggest. These aspects will be treated in Chapter 8 where I will propose an interpretation of organizational decision-making as everyday life practice using the lens of social phenomenology.

# 3
# From Theory to Empirical Research

In the first part of the book I have outlined the theoretical background that served as a basis for the empirical research performed. It must be said, however, that the process has been dynamic, since the research itself has informed the choice of the theoretical aspects that were more relevant for the research. Of course not all the literature analyzed makes an appearance in these chapters, and not all the literature presented is directly related to the research. I wanted to give voice also to certain aspects such as the Russian formalists definitions, over Ricoeur's narrative time articulation, as although they will not explicitly appear in the second and third part of the book they were nevertheless important for the evolution of my research and for the general contribution they have provided in the field.

Chapter 1 opened with the definition of narrative as provided by narratologists and the work of Russian formalists. Such definitions are in my view important as they represent a reference point for every scholar interested in narrative research. There is also a bibliographical aspect in this incipit, as my fascination for stories started during elementary school when we studied an exemplified version of Propp's analysis of folktales. The idea of the hero leaving home, encountering all sorts of difficulties and finally solving them was a very reassuring pattern for a nine-year-old child.

Although the focus of the work is in organizational stories, I wanted to step back, in the first chapter, to the work of the scholars that had studied narratives in the literature and philosophy realm. I would find out that no consensus is reached between their definition and the ones provided by social sciences scholars. The narrative definition provided by narratologists has to do with the temporal development and the mechanisms through which chronological sequence relates to the time-space continuum created by the narrator. Russian formalists identify two different instances in the narrative notion: *fabula* for the events in their chronological sequence and *syzhet* for the events in the order presented in the text (these two aspects will be assimilated with the notion of story and discourse). This definition can be hardly applicable in my view to social sciences research where narratives are treated as empirically observable actions, rather than texts. Genette identifies a third instance: together with narrated content and the account of such content, the act of the telling should be located (although in his view is still internal to the text).

Herrnstein Smith amended the definition of narrative by relaxing the core aspect of temporal reconstruction in favor of a definition of narrative as someone who tells someone else that something happened.

The narrative definition provided by formalists raises an important issue, that of personal and unique reinterpretation process operated by the subject. To address this issue Ricoeur uses the notion of narrative time as the inscription of phenomenological time on cosmological time. For Ricoeur, narrative represents the basic structure of our experience of time.

Narrative definition in organizational realm has been integrated by socio-constructionist views to detect the ways events are plotted within organizational settings. If plot organizes events and makes sense of otherwise unconnected instances, it must be noticed that it is historically and socially constructed.

One question running through the book and partially addressed in the second and third parts is: what is left of what there was before the plotting into narratives? Boje's concept of antenarrative aims directly at this point: antenarrative is what is there before narrative, and a bet against it. It is to me the space outside the plot. But narratives are also practices, in the sense of Genette's act of the telling and Herrnstein Smith's definition, and are influenced by the immediate situation of the telling. Narratives are both influenced and contribute to influencing such contexts.

In the first chapter I chose to include Bakhtin's articulation of the social and relational orientation of the utterance as it is of paramount importance in the detecting of what the consolidated narratives within the organizational context considered are and how they are recounted.

However, in the first chapter instances are introduced that cannot be reconciled to what is defined by Bakhtin as we-experience, an ideological form derived from social relations. Individuals are always already in dialogic relations with both mediated and disruptive forms to which they are socially oriented, in a chain of infinite combinations. Storytelling, and in particular conversational storytelling, is thus an active and dynamic attempt that can never be final or proper such as in the formalist understanding. Storytelling does not reflect a finalized world: storytelling creates such world.

This aspect is at the basis of the radical shift that has made it possible for narrative to enter the field of social sciences. Social sciences and management sciences (among the last ones) have in the last 30 years been informed by what is known as linguistic turn. If language becomes a constituent of society instead of a way to report on it, social phenomena may as well be studied using language-based interpretations. In addition, narrative knowledge has been recognized as an alternative mode of knowing and not in contrast with scientific knowledge. As Lyotard pointed out, along with scientific knowledge narrative knowledge must be recognized.

Postmodern thinkers such as Vattimo have argued that accepting such a fragmentation of paradigm will provide us with the light of a different attitude. Stories may not be necessarily a way of achieving truth but they can shed light on how people find a *modus vivendi* with truth.

Away from the desire of creating grand theories, narrative researchers look for the particular and contingent meanings. The way of engaging with research is different in the narrative paradigm and, as expressed by Clandinin, experience is the fundamental ontological category of narrative research.

In the second part of the book, and particularly in the fourth chapter, you will find examples of how the observer/field dichotomy is not applicable to narrative research. The second part of the book is called *Research Experience* to emphasize the experiential dimension of fieldwork.

In the second chapter I have provided an overview of narrative inquiry in organizational research giving an historical outline, starting with the works of Clark in 1972 and of Mitroff and Kilmann in 1975. As said in the beginning of this section, not all the literature of the field has been presented but rather the works that relate most closely to the work that I have done.

It was important nevertheless to point out that narrative research in the organizational domain is not a unitary body of work, and different authors have used different definitions of story/narrative, different epistemological foundations, different methodologies and have studied different aspects of organizational life.

Narrative research encompasses both studies of stories collected in organizations and studies of organizations as narrative texts or even organization theory as a form of narrative itself. The focus of the organizational literature review has been the studies of story-telling organizations, through the stories that are told within orga-nizations and the stories that organizations create (official speeches, brochures, advertisement and so on).

My empirical research is primarily focused on the conversational storytelling performed by the managers, but references to material sources and their relationships to the oral accounts are also provided.

Several authors have dealt with storytelling organizations; among them I would cite the work of Professor Barbara Czarniawska, Pro-fessor Yannis Gabriel and Professor David Boje, with whom I had the honor to perform my empirical research. I believe these three authors are the key players where storytelling organization's insights are concerned.

In the second chapter I have analyzed the work published by Boje in 1991 as well as the work done by Gabriel in the same year. Boje has studied spontaneous storytelling at an office supply firm, arguing that storytelling is the preferred sense-making currency in human relations within organizations, and that the stories people tell do not have a full plot but are told in bits and pieces. He has also argued that the study of storytelling must be paired with the study of how stories are abbreviated and how much of the story is told or how much is exaggerated. These aspects, called terse storytelling and glossing, are part of the endeavor of complementing the study of stories as text with the study of stories as performances.

Gabriel in 1991 also published a study about the collection of spontaneous stories in different work and military organizations. For Gabriel, stories are a way to cope with pain and to make the organization a livable place. They open a window into the emotional and symbolic lives of organizations: they perform a soothing function.

One interesting question that arises is about the different functions that stories and storytelling performs in organizations. Boje's examples can be connected to communitarian function (referring to Jedlowski's notation) in the cited work of 1991 or they can become social control devices as in the case of the stories of Walt Disney and the Magic Kingdom. In his Disney study, published in 1995, Boje takes a much more critical view on storytelling by showing how official narratives were paired with counter-narratives of marginal or excluded stories of strikes, reprimands and Tayloristic practices.

The cited work by Orr of 1996 shows us yet another function that narratives can perform: that of training and providing practical instruction on how to solve problems when no other information is available. The war stories that Orr's copy machine technicians tell to each other represent a way to sort out information in order to determine the diagnosis of the problem encountered.

Orr's example also fits with what was my initial object of study: decision-making. This object has been changed over the duration of the research as a result of the impressive interviews that I had with the bankers. In a way the object has been changed by the research itself. In the third part you will find an entire chapter devoted to decision-making and how it relates to the empirical research and the result obtained.

In the second chapter I devoted a paragraph to the two examples that I found most fitting for my research sensitivity, although I repeat the research has not been conducted in these terms. The contribution provided by the two examples is that narrative can serve as a guide for decision-making as in the case of Orr, or as an ex-post legitimation as in the case of O'Connor. The war stories of Orr also contribute to the way technicians see their profession and thus perform a strong identitarian function.

These were actually some of the questions that I asked myself at several points during my research: what are the stories of the bankers I will be interviewing? What types of functions will they solve and what is the role of such stories in the bankers' everyday working life? But also in line with Boje's critical interest: what are the stories that the bank wants to tell? And, how can I detect narratives and antenarratives in the bankers' accounts? Also, more generally, how do living stories differ from the narratives defined by formalists? And, what relations do they hold with such narratives? What are the functions of storytelling in such organization?

Again I must recall that this work is written in slightly reverse order since the first part has been shaped after field research and so when entering field research not all the theoretical aspects where present in the order and with the importance given in these chapters.

# Part II

# Research Experience

# 4
# Methodology and Methods

> Narrative inquiry is a way of understanding experience. It is collaboration between researcher and participants, over time, in a place or series of places, and in social interaction with milieus. An inquirer enter this matrix in the midst and progresses in the same spirit, concluding the inquiry still in the midst of living and telling, reliving and retelling, the stories of the experiences that made up people's lives, both individual and social.
>
> (Clandinin and Connelly, 2000, p. 20)

As I said before, it is interesting noticing, talking about story reconstruction, that this work is written in slightly reverse order compared to the actual chronological flow of the work. There are rules in writing for academic research, as well as a genre. The first two chapters were developed during the third year of my PhD in Lugano, while the second and most of the third part of the work were developed in New Mexico and in the months that immediately followed my return. The first part of the work was then shaped after my return from New Mexico in order to give importance to the aspects that were more closely related to the research. Nevertheless, when I left for New Mexico I knew I wanted to use Boje's narrative understanding and methodology and I was fascinated by the idea of applying such an intriguing concept in the empirical work, but I had no idea of how and where this could have been possible. The idea was that of investigating the relationship between decision-making and organizational narratives. It was an idea conceived in the first two years of my PhD when I was involved in a project on knowledge communication in decision-making context: unsatisfied by the lack of social and relational understanding of many knowledge communication approaches, I started to investigate on my own alternative paradigms that could shed light on such a complex matter. The initial idea of investigating decision-making is still present in this book although it does not hold a primary role. As will be discussed in this chapter, the empirical research itself has shaped and readdressed the object of the research.

The story of this chapter is thus not only a story of how and where but also of whom; the who are Professor Boje and Professor Loveland and the bankers that made this research possible. For the specificity of the work and the paradigm used I will provide a number of biographical aspects that are usually omitted in other types of research but become relevant in this discourse.

## 4.1  Entering the field – John Loveland

I arrived in Las Cruces in the end of August 2006, after spending one year thinking about and researching the idea of narrative in organizational research. In the previous two years, together with the course requirements for the PhD, I was involved in a project on knowledge communication between decision makers and experts in the realm of management. It was actually during those years that I developed most of the critical thoughts on some research in the field. Neither studying organizations nor banking institutions were new for me, as many of the decision makers interviewed during the two years of the project were either from banking institutions or connected with the financial service industry. Also, in the two years prior to my enrollment as a PhD student I was working in consulting company PricewaterhouseCoopers, where I served as a junior consultant in the financial services practice team. I had the chance to be an assistant on a big project regarding the centralization of the treasury functions between four banks of the same group, with all the implications from an accounting, organizational and information system point of view.

Being a junior consultant I had no experience of direct interviews with the professionals of the bank, which was the task of the higher ranks in the firm to whom I reported. Since the job was done mainly on the premises of the clients in Siena (Tuscany) and far away from the office in Milan, it was a custom to dine and spend time together before returning to the hotel. It was actually during those hours of collective diversion that a great number of stories about the meetings circulated.

Although it was second hand experience, it was very powerful. There is a jargon, a style and even a mood that I can still now associate with the professionals of the financial services, starting from that particular experience. It was mainly for these reasons that when I arrived in Las Cruces in 2006 I felt that I wanted to do some local empirical research in a banking institution. Although the context of New Mexico had little to do with my previous experience, I felt that I was comfortable enough with banking to be able to do narrative research in the field.

I must admit that in the days after my arrival in Las Cruces, I felt quite lost. The city is very different from the European cities in which I had lived and it seemed to me so vast and inaccessible for somebody who did not have a car. Wells Fargo Bank was just behind my house, the house that I had rented with a masters student from Ecuador, Pamela, who studied in the Agricultural Department, the biggest and most important at New Mexico State University. Just across the street from our house, stood the department and next to it, the barns.

Khadija, the Moroccan PhD student also working with Professor Boje, advised me to open my account at Wells Fargo, pictured in Figure 4.1, saying that it was very close to my apartment. The next day I left my house but walked in the opposite direction, wandering around the bull's barn looking for the bank. I gave up and went back home. The next day I found the bank; one of the entrances to the bank was in the exact apartment complex I was living in.

The bank teller was very nice and after opening the account I told him that I was doing research on the bank and wanted to know a little bit more about the history of the bank. He told me to call him the next day and when I did so, he gave me the name of the president of the commercial bank and his secretary. I called the secretary and she gave me an appointment for the next week on 11 September.

The idea of saying that I wanted to know more of the history of the bank was that of Professor Boje, he knew I wanted to study the relation between storytelling and decision-making practices but he feared that asking about decision-making would not foster storytelling, if we wanted to hear stories we would have to start with the simplest

*Figure 4.1*   Wells Fargo bank on El Paseo. (Picture taken by Marisa Ortman.)

story: that of the bank, all the other stories would come spontaneously afterwards. This strategy has shown great results, to the point that the focus of the research has changed over the time, since the material had opened such interesting paths that it was reductive to focus on decision-making practices. However, I will come back to this aspect later.

The interesting part is that I dived into research before knowing what would emerge and without having finished writing the first part of the work, with no hypothesis. Professor Boje forced me to enter the organizational empirical world collecting every kind of material: he asked me to collect brochures in the lobby of the bank, to analyze the logo, to talk to people in the bank, or customers waiting in the line, anything.

If it was not for him, I would probably still be in search of a good case to construct for my empirical research. Thanks to him I realized that the good case was in my own back yard.

I think all this and what I will tell you afterwards is very important when we talk about the methodology of research. It deals with a specific sensitivity and a way to engage with research that is perfectly fitting with the idea of constant dialog of the researcher with all the objects, signs and discourses that constitutes our everyday life. It is for this reason that these paragraphs look more like a journal than a methodology chapter.

I feel that this ties also to the more general vision of continuity between the observed reality and the researcher rather than a separation between the two. It is a view that has been exposed already in the first chapter and which is central to the whole organization of the book and represents also a sensitivity that permeates the whole research.

In this sense stories become living stories, not only because they have movement, they are alive as Boje has argued and in the sense that Jo Tyler (a member of the Storytelling Organization Institute led by Prof. Boje), is now researching, but also because they have to do with our lives, they overlap with the stories in which we are immersed in various ways and at various levels. What I am going to tell you next will illustrate what I am saying more clearly.

The day after the interview with the president of the commercial bank, I was reporting on it to Professor Boje. We were in the Frenger Court, one of the college canteens and Professor Boje seeing another Professor sitting next to our table invited him to join us. He introduced him to me as Professor John Loveland, who I later learned is an institution at New Mexico State University.

Boje asked him about banking in Las Cruces and told him I was doing research in that area. Not only was Professor Loveland very knowledgeable about the history of banking in Las Cruces but he also personally knows the most prominent figures of the banking industry in Las Cruces. He told us the story of when he first arrived in Las Cruces and needed a car loan: John Papen was one of his students and introduced him to the bank. "John Papen is the nephew of Frank Papen, the one that built the tower, downtown", Professor Loveland told us. He also briefly sketched the history of the bank, from the First National Bank of Dona Ana County, and the transition into "another bank, I don't remember the name" and Wells Fargo. He spoke about the act that made it possible for national banks to branch outside their state.

Some days later I was in Professor Loveland's office, writing down names and telephone numbers. He asked me to go to the dean's office and look at the distinguished alumni plates on the wall. I called John Papen, the interview was scheduled and I was entering the field: no hypothesis; no questionnaire; no chapter three and no idea of what that interview would open up in terms of research.

## 4.2   Las Cruces and First National Bank – the book

There is a bookstore in downtown Las Cruces where they sell used books and where they have a section on the local history. Hidden on the shelves there were three copies of a book called *Southern New Mexico Empire: The First National Bank of Dona Ana County* by Leon Metz. I opened the introduction where a few words are devoted to its beginning as a mortgage bank dealing in land investment and alfalfa, and fruits for the first 15 years and cotton later.

I began to write in my notebook, "The bank has nurtured cattle-men, immigrants, businesses, colleges and the government" (Metz, 1991, xi), and continued reading:

> Without the First National, Elephant Butte Dam and the New Mexico State University might not have reached their present status as superior institutions. The people who accepted leadership roles in encouraging the dam and the school where the same ones who organized the bank. Strong and magnetic individuals have guided the bank since its creation...however the story of First National Bank of Dona Ana County is more than a record of dividends and interest rates, of loan paid off and mortgages that struggled. A bank is people...bank employees have served in elected offices, they have sat on the federal, state and local, civic and professional boards. They have attended church and public meetings. They have managed business. Most have had backgrounds and educations fitting them to be bankers. Some have been better equipped than others...The history of First National Bank of Dona Ana County is a narrative of regional growth, of how an obscure bank rose to prominence during the Twentieth Century. The saga of the First National Bank of Dona Ana County, New Mexico, is the chronicle of a leader.
>
> (Metz, 1991, xi–xii)

I bought the book and rode my bike home.

The interesting aspect is that I bought and read this book before knowing that John Papen and the banker I had interviewed from Wells Fargo were related, and actually this was even before John Loveland introduced me to John Papen.

Anyway, I remember very well the eve of my interview with John Papen. At that time I was reading *Telling Decisions* by O'Connor (1996) trying to figure out what to ask John Papen about decisions. However, I got distracted as I started looking at the pictures of the presidents of the bank in Leon Metz's book and read a good part of the book. I realized I was starting to get involved in the research in a different way. I was starting to realize that I was opening myself to the place and the people that had shaped it and had been shaped by it.

There is a constant reference to the places in the book and in the words of the people I would later on interview: there is reference to the University, in which most of them had studied and had entered in various occasions with different titles and for different purposes: that university was the same university I was enrolled at and where Boje works; the weather they spoke about, the hostile floods and the nice climate was the same weather that I was experiencing myself, the heavy rain when I arrived in August and the wonderful autumn warmth. The tower would become a point of reference for me in Las Cruces, I would see the tower every time I would ride my bike downtown or every Monday and Wednesday afternoon when gathering for an informal meeting with Professor Boje from the window of his office on the third floor of the Business Complex.

A few days later, I rode my bike downtown to visit the Thomas Branigan Memorial Library, and spent time reading about First National Bank in a book called *Las Cruces, New Mexico, 1849–1999, Multicultural Crossroads* by Gordon Owen. I started to recognize the stories, the characters and the places, the Elephant Butte Dam, Oscar Snow being the "alfalfa king", Papen as "Mr First National" and the tower and so on.

I also started reading books that had little to do with the research, but once the interest was activated is was very difficult to stop. I found myself on the floor of the Library reading another book, *Shalam – Utopia on the Rio Grande 1881–1907*. It is the story of the Shalam colony for the orphans and the abandoned: the story of the failure of a utopian experiment by two men that arrived in 1884 at the Amador Hotel in this "men less land waiting for landless men". Few months later during a hike in the mountain I think I even saw what still exists of the old colony.

## 4.3   The first interview – John Papen

When I entered John Papen's office, I did not know that this interview would change the course of my entire research, and the future of my interests as a researcher.

I remember waiting for Professor Boje in front of my house on a sunny (there are no gloomy days in the south of New Mexico) autumn morning thinking to myself "I should present my research first. I should tell him what the purpose is. I should tell him that I want to show whether a relationship exists between storytelling and decision-making". I opened my notebook and wrote it down. I say this because I think it is important to notice that even in my own experience as a researcher I faced the same exact tension that I have observed in my research, the tension between what is already structured and what is emergent. And for this reason I say that the interview with John Papen was crucial, as it proved it possible to encounter such tension in the field and in such a deep and fascinating way.

During the interview, John Papen talked about the bank, about his uncle and about his colleagues in a way that was almost like being in a movie. Later on I asked myself whether the older generations have a natural ability toward storytelling that is lost in my generation or in the generation of the younger bankers that I have interviewed. This could be one of the reasons, but I don't think it is the only explanation for that unique storytelling performance by John Papen. In the last chapter I will treat some of the themes that I think are the most relevant for explaining different types of organizational storytelling as performed by both the old managing team of the First National Bank of Dona Ana and the new managing team for the Las Cruces area for Wells Fargo (I say the Las Cruces area because unlike First National Bank of Dona Ana which was a local independent bank, Wells Fargo is a nationwide bank in which the southern New Mexico is a only part). At this stage I would like to show how the research unfolded and why I consider the encounter with John Papen that day so precious for my research.

First of all, the storytelling was almost spontaneous; Professor Boje provoked it with few words placed a very delicate way. I recollect that from the very beginning I realized that the stories John Papen was going to tell us were dense with people, moments and dates that had particular significance to him. It was in that moment that I fully understood the sense of fragmented stories, with no beginning, middle and end, which Boje had talked about throughout his research, and his idea of living stories and the storytelling of his grandmother Wilda – of one of his lectures. I could have asked John

Papen formal questions about decision-making, and he did talk about decision-making but in such a different way that I felt there was no sense in taking the approach I had in the previous interview with the president of the commercial bank, and with the bankers that I had interviewed in Switzerland on the project on knowledge communication.

During those previous interviews, and also in the one I had made in Las Cruces by myself, few stories had emerged. Here we were listening to John Papen's experience as a banker in Las Cruces. It was very different; it was a radical shift. Without the coaching of Professor Boje I could have never made this shift.

Months later I found that Barbara Czarniawska in her *Narrating the Organization: Dramas of Institutional Identity* (1997) talks about the same problem:

> Trained in "scientific" techniques of data collecting, I tended to structure my interviews along usual analytical lines my interest in the narrative notwithstanding. "What are the most acute problems you are facing today?" and "Can you compare your situation with that of two years ago?" are questions that will raise no eyebrows; researchers ask people in the field to compare to abstract, to generalize. Some of my interlocutors would bravely engage in the logical exercise I demanded, but most would break through my structure, saying "Let me tell you how all it started" or "You need some background first". Upon which they would engage in producing a rich narrative, which might or might not be finally summarized along the lines I had suggested. This used to bring me to the verge of panic – "How to bring them to the point?" – whereas now I have at least learned that this is the point.
>
> (Czarniawska, 1997a, p. 28)

Also, from a theoretical point of view, it was thanks to the interview with John Papen that I started to approach Ricoeur's philosophy and to fully understand the tension between experience and the appropriation of time when recollecting events.

There has been a shift during the work toward a phenomenological approach that could take into account the experience of people working in organizations and its relation with the storytelling performed;

the focus on decision-making has slowly faded. In this sense it can be said that the first interview with John Papen has shown the possibility of studying organizational storytelling through the lens of personal experience. Toward the end of the interview, and actually also in some moments during the interview, we experienced strong emotional tension and energy that had no semantic configuration but yet was there. In the Chapter 7 I will situate it between an anticipation of a loss that nevertheless occurs when the social dimension comes into play in its reductive terms and an excess of sense that will be always overlapping in the "storied" accounts.

Later in the interviews I started noticing pauses, silences, drumming of fingers, changes of the facial expression that accompanied those moments. I started to understand that two different types of storytelling were apparent: stories that were more organized and collectively produced and stories that were more fragmented and personal.

The role of the researcher is crucial at this point, as the relational aspect of storytelling is paramount. "An interviewer who presents himself or herself either as too deeply committed to those interests and that order or as clearly outside of them, restricts which cultural stories interviewees may tell and how these will be told" (Miller and Glassner, 2001, p. 130). Cultural stories are defined following Richardson as "told from the point of view of the ruling interests and the normative order" (Richardson, 1990, p. 25). What I want to say here is that the researcher has to be aware of the commitment issue involved in narrative interviews. The way he or she is perceived will affect the storytelling performed.

The next chapter will be devoted to the content of the interviews, great emphasis will be given to the excerpts of interviews: here I want to highlight the overall effect arising from them.

## 4.4   Collecting stories

As I said before, my engagement with this research changed dramatically after meeting Professor Loveland, the interview with John Papen and during the reading of the book on the bank. Beside the interviews, I searched for every way to come into contact with stories regarding the bank, doing ethnographic research in my daily life in Las Cruces, collecting brochures, journal articles and talking to people in different social situations. I consider this material, although only partially expressed in this work, an important constituent of it.

I have talked already about the excess of sense that the world holds compared to any account; here you can find an application of this. What you will find in the next chapter are the quotations from some of the transcribed interviews, from the book written by Leon Metz, from the newsletters and brochures, and official meetings. The landscape of my research holds for me an excess of sense compared to these texts.

In the first interview with John Papen he provided me with the newsletters of the First National Bank of Dona Ana, which I photocopied before returning to him at our second interview. They were very rich materials, which really made me feel closer to what life was like at First National Bank: their involvement in the community; the friendly atmosphere of parties and trips; the reward given to employees and so on. John Papen also gave me a thick book full of articles regarding the bank and his uncle, his honorary degrees and awards.

In the Rio Grande Historical Collection at New Mexico State University I had access to Leon Metz's research files, which included interviews with Frank Papen and many of the people that I was interviewing at the time, letters and materials gathered by the author. Interestingly I also had access to the minutes of the board meetings of First National Bank of Dona Ana that were donated by First Security Corporation to the Collection after their acquisition. It is extraordinary material, which requires refined understanding of deliberation at board meetings, having a language and a style of its own. For this reason it represents a stylistic discourse that can be compared dialogically with the conversational storytelling of the interviews. I had never seen minutes of board meetings before (and probably will never have the chance again) and it took me a good 15 minutes simply to understand how to read the books. They are made in a way that once a new book is open then minutes are inserted and in the next meeting the minutes are inserted on the top of the others which means that only in the end they are all tied together and the book is closed. This means that if you open the book you will find the last board meeting first and so it appears in a reverse chronological order. Studying narrative I already find this part fascinating.

I had access to Leon Metz research files several times, but the minutes I only saw once. When I reported to Professor Boje that First Security Corporation had donated the minutes of Board Meetings of First National Bank of Dona Ana to the University, we realized how interesting it would have been to triangulate the interviews and the storytelling with the written minutes, which are the ultimate written storytelling of the bank. But, unfortunately when Professor Boje and I asked formally to spend time in the archives to analyze these minutes, they did not give us permission: but that is another story.

## 4.5   Research interviews

In Chapter 5 are extracts of the interviews I have carried out with the bankers throughout my stay in Las Cruces. The first interview with John Papen was a long, unstructured interview of about two hours and all the interviews I had thereafter were of the same format. I interviewed John Papen several times, and the same can be said for all the interviewees.

The interviewees can be divided into two different sets. The first set is that of the people that belonged to the First National Bank of Dona Ana, the original group: the CEO, the CFO and the Vice President of the bank. These three people were the managing team of the bank for several years and together faced the transition into First Security Corporation, first, and later into Wells Fargo. Only one of them is still working for the bank. He still maintains his office in the tower where he cherishes the memories of a lifelong work experience. I always met him in that office, while I've met the others on different premises: the University and a meeting room of one of the Wells Fargo branches.

The second set is that of managers of Wells Fargo bank that were not involved with First National Bank prior to the First Security Corporation acquisition. Their age range is different and their ties with the community are also different. They all came from previous working experiences within the Wells Fargo bank and other banks in different locations from Las Cruces but mostly in the New-Mexico/Texas area. In the fifth chapter you will find in parenthesis after each excerpt symbols like A1, B1, C1, D2 and E2. The letters correspond to the different interviewees and make it easier for the reader to identify them, the numbers indicate whether they belong to the first set or second set (former First National Bank identified with 1 and Wells Fargo identified with 2).

I have made long unstructured interviews with both sets, recorded materials and transcribed materials for an overall effort of more than 200 hours including the preparation of the interviews, the actual recording, the transcriptions and the editing. The interviews were made between September 2006 and April 2007 in Las Cruces, New Mexico. The excerpts you will find in the fifth chapter are only one small portion of the materials I have gathered. I also decided to concentrate my attention on the few interviews that I found to be more interesting and rich from a narrative point of view. It has been a conscious choice to concentrate on a few individuals and to go into depth on several aspects of their working lives, instead of doing a more superficial work on a larger basis. The interviews that are reported here are just the tip of the iceberg compared to the interactions I had with the bankers and the research I did. Not all the conversations were taped; some of the conversations that were made when the tape recorder was turned off actually contain aspects that are fundamental to understanding the entire research. Such aspects are all noted in the two notebooks that I always carried with me, pictured in Figure 4.2, and that are part of the research itself. The consultation of the archives at the Rio Grande Historical Collection and at the Branigan Library are also part of this endeavor and are commented on in the notebooks, as well as the journal articles and observation at the bank, looking at the pictures and posters, listening to conversations between employees, taking a ride home from the bank with the secretary of the vice president and so on. In the notebook you can find the notes of the interviews, the comments on them on the left side, the notes on the archival researches, the comments on the articles read on the bank, the comments on the visits at the bank and so on.

In the second chapter I have talked about the specificities of narrative research, I must add here that one aspect of narrative research is also the innovative format of the presentation of the research result. In any case it is important here to point out that nine people were the subject of the interviews. The formal interviews (taped and two hours long) regard only five people on two or three occasions of an overall 14 interviews and part of these 14 interviews are the excerpts that you will find in the next chapter.

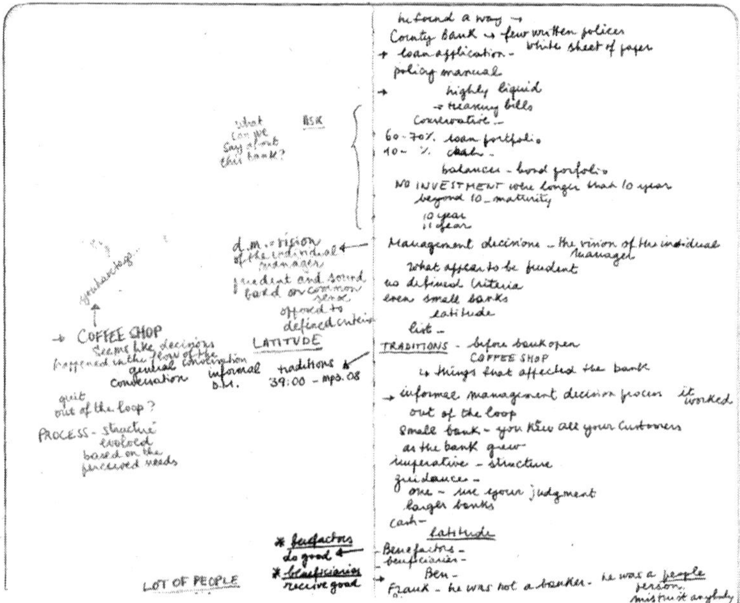

*Figure 4.2*   A sample page from my notebooks.

The transcribed materials are extremely rich and difficult to manage. There are software packages that can be useful in this sense and I used the NVivo software although mainly for archival purposes. I taped the entire conversations we had with the bankers and transcribed every part of them: they were informal interviews in the form of a conversation (see Figure 4.3 for an image of the tape recorder used). For every hour of conversation it took me about five hours to transcribe and on average seven hours to get to the edited text.

Transcription is a crucial part in the research. I transcribed my interviews immediately after I had taped them, I found it useful since the memories of the events are still fresh and it's easier to recollect what happened behind the talking. I find the listening to the interviews always richer than the written text and for this reason sometime I also listen to them after the transcription.

As I said before, I transcribed every interview on the same day that I made it, often taking me more than one day to transcribe

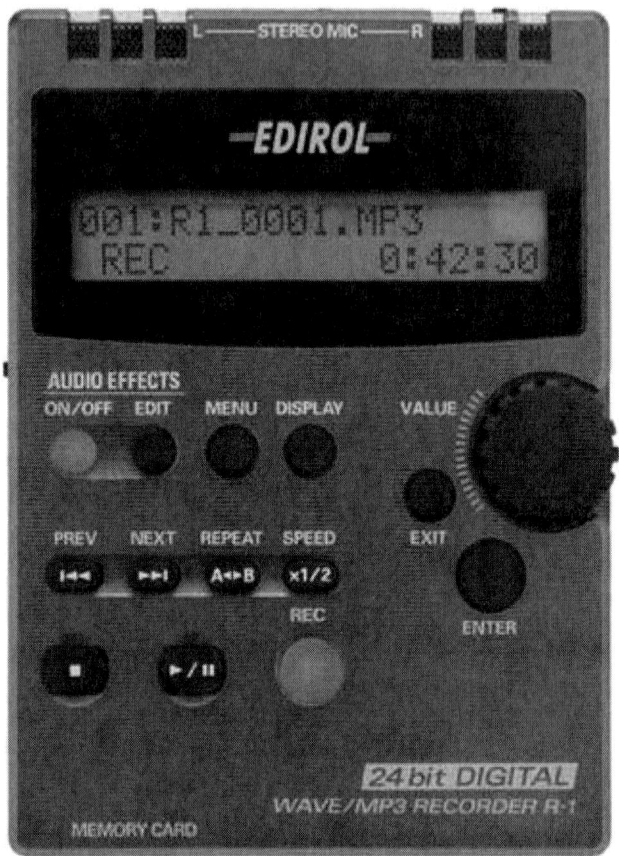

*Figure 4.3*  Professor Boje's tape recorder I used for the interviews.

an interview. This allowed me to get acquainted with the material before the next interview, to read the manuscript several times, after listening to it many times.

I have a way of transcribing that although less efficient I think can be very useful in the kind of research I have been doing. I listen to the tape once to recollect the general idea of the interview. Then I start transcribing, stopping the tape after every sentence, even though there are words that I don't understand, and I go on like this.

I never rewind the tape and go back just to listen to a single word again. When I am done with the first draft, I listen to the tape again (I use the word tape even though they are files that are transferred from the digital recorder to the computer) and fill in the blanks. If there are words that it is really impossible to understand I bring the transcript with me to the following interview and I ask the interviewees whether he can recollect that passage (I can use the word "he" because I only have males as interviewees).

What is the idea behind the no rewind rule? Nobody really tells you how to transcribe texts and you are basically self-taught on the subject, there are some disciplines that require very strict rules in transcribing with a strong notation to learn. Conversational analysts for example use a standardized set of symbols to make it easier to understand what the original conversation could have been. Organizational studies interviews are often transcribed partially by the researcher, and sometimes not even transcribed. In a work on conversational storytelling I felt that the transcription needed to be as precise as possible, putting it down word for word, and marking down situational aspects as well. I used some of the symbols used by conversational analysts like capital letters to indicate a word or a phrase louder than the regular level of speech or putting in double parentheses a description of some phenomena that characterized the words or the scene. For more extensive references on conversation analysis, see Boden and Zimmerman (1991). On the other hand I did not note for example, as conversational analysts do, elapsed time in tenths of a second, slight gaps or prolonged syllables. We have to remember also that most of the conversations transcribed are not spontaneous conversations and thus could not be eligible for strict conversation analysis methodology. For this reason I would say that the technique used is quite personal and the freedom I was able to use in the methodology reflects the fact that there is no common understanding between narrative analysis researchers. It can be said that my method reflects my interest in showing voices and movement, so if one reads the interviews one has the impression of reading the script for a piece of theater or a screenplay, which of course is made after the scene is already performed. Since I wanted to stress the performance aspect of storytelling I never wanted to rewind, I thought that by doing so I would have loosened the thought flow of the interviewees.

## 4.6   Narrative research

Narrative methodology is a very broad term that encompasses distant and heterogeneous research paths, mostly under the qualitative research umbrella. Qualitative research is not mainstream in the managerial domain, although it is becoming more and more well received. The divide between quantitative and qualitative research is not about whether or not numbers are used but rather the engagement and the goals of the research are different.

Denzin and Lincoln (1994) start their *Handbook of Qualitative Research* with the following definition:

> Qualitative research is multimethod in focus, involving an interpretive naturalistic approach to its subject matter...qualitative researchers study things in their natural settings attempting to make sense of, or interpret, phenomena in terms of the meanings people bring to them. Qualitative research involves the studied use of and collection of a variety of empirical materials...that describe routine and problematic moments and meaning in individuals' lives.
>
> (pp. 2)

Narrative research cannot be unified under the same paradigm and often researchers that describe themselves as narrative researcher use very different approaches and strategies when dealing with empirical materials. I also agree with Pinnegar and Daynes (2006) when they say "Narrative researchers use narrative in some way in their research. Narrative inquiry embraces narrative as both the method and phenomena of study" (Pinnegar and Daynes, 2006, pp. 4–5).

Moreover the narrative methodology has been exploratory in the organizational domain as in every cross-border discipline. The methodology I used for analyzing the material and engaging with the research subjects cannot be restricted to one unitary paradigm. Different influences and sometimes even spontaneous improvisation made this research possible. The opportunity to conduct research in New Mexico has made it possible to benefit from Professor Boje's impressive knowledge on narrative methodology. Boje has guided me through the interviews, being present at most of them and he assisted in the analysis.

As recollected in Chapter 2, Boje has made important contributions to the field of narrative inquiry and collected stories of and within organizations such as Disney, Stew Leonard, McDonald, Wal-Mart, Nike and Enron. My research has been influenced by the two cited works of 1991 and 1994, the first about the spontaneous stories collected at the office supply firm and the second about the official storytelling of the Disney organization, and his book of 2001 *Narrative Methods for Organizational and Communication Research*, where he argues in favor of antenarrative research and explains possible research paths to engage in such a research.

The methodology used is also informed by the specificity of the theories that have influenced me throughout the research, in particular Professor Jedlowski's sensitivity toward the phenomenological tradition with a great concern on the experience of the self and memory in the contemporary society. This is why I would insist on defining the methodology exploratory, because although there existed examples of previous research in organization, I tried also to integrate notions and concepts that were not together linked to the managerial realm.

# 5
# Las Cruces: Stories from a Southwestern Bank

In this chapter you will find excerpts from the transcripts of the interviews with the bankers, Leon Metz's book, newsletters, brochures, archival materials and personal comments edited into seven sections: beginning; Frank Papen; decision-makers; acquisitions; new life and new bankers.

At this stage I wanted to give voice to the material, rather than make conclusions about the work. Nevertheless the excerpts are briefly commented on through the use of theoretical aspects already considered in the previous chapters; reflections stemming from this work and informing narrative inquiry will be discussed in the following chapter.

The material you will find is just a small portion compared to the analyzed material, especially in terms of transcribed interviews. The background is a story of a community bank in the town of Las Cruces that having been managed in a certain way for a number of years, has undergone in the last ten years two different acquisitions, becoming part of a larger network.

Along with the supporting material, you will find in this chapter five main voices, divided in two groups, the first group is that of the old managers of the bank and the second group is that of the new managers for the Las Cruces area.

Please note that the excerpts are from transcriptions of conversational storytelling, sometimes you may find "( )" when the tape was not clear or "…" when people are pausing or when there is a jump to a different topic: what is possible in conversation may seem difficult to read when written, so I ask the reader to make an effort in this sense. Between double parentheses "(( ))" you may find nonverbal aspects that accompanied the storytelling, such as laughing or pondering. When a sentence is capitalized it means a higher volume of the voice or greater emphasis by the interviewee.

Letters distinguish the voices, so that a different person corresponds to each letter. After each letter there is a number, which highlights which group the voice is from. The first group is that of the bankers who have been in the bank through the acquisitions and the second group is that of the new comers.

These voices are telling stories, which intertwine with the stories of the bank and are accompanied by other stories found in the different materials above mentioned. The result is a story in itself, not completed, not final but rather fragmented and dynamic. This story doesn't show one place and one time, but rather the different places and times of the worlds created by each and every account.

Here is the incipit of the historian's account on the bank:

I first visited Las Cruces, New Mexico in 1948 when the town was tiny and basically devoid of streetlights and activity. Surrounding towns were quaint, but Las Cruces seemed without a form, a huddle of adobe buildings separated by narrow streets, many of them unpaved.

(Metz, 1991, p. xi)

It is Leon Metz talking in the introduction of his book *Southern New Mexico Empire*. The landscape he describes is a very different landscape compared to the one it opens to the view of the visitor nowadays: Las Cruces is a big university town, with wide streets, lights and commercial activities (see Figure 5.1). It is not the purpose of this chapter to tell the history of the town, although constant references will be made. As I said in the previous chapter, the story of the research, my personal experience of this place and the stories of the bankers that will be voiced in this chapter are intertwined with their experience of the place that they have contributed to shaping and by which they have been shaped.

*Figure 5.1*   Las Cruces 2007, the bank taken from Alameda. (Picture taken by Marisa Ortman.)

Here is an extract from one of the interviews, where one of the bankers invites me to read a passage from another book written on another western bank:

Well, I thought, before we started you may be interested in looking at a paragraph or two here...It's a case of history repeating itself, just start right here...(From A History of a Western Bank, Paul Rader) *Fate was to deal Pat Campbell another harsh blow. The Bank of Hatch nicely survived the 1920 recession and the slow fading away of fluorspar mining, but it was not to survive Mother Nature. On August 17, 1921, after a night of torrential cloudbursts, the Placitas Arroyo that funneled into Hatch brought down a wall of water that destroyed the adobe-constructed bank, Pat's home, and most of Hatch as well. Looking over the ruins in a state of dejection, Pat realized that neither the bank nor Hatch itself could recover except over an agonizingly long period of time. Reestablishing the bank elsewhere was the only answer. Pat turned his eyes back to Las Cruces.*

See that's exactly the same thing that happened up there this summer, except that it didn't destroyed banks, but it did destroy a lot of buildings, same Arroyo, almost the same time, I think the floods probably occurred a few week earlier this year ... (B1).

I arrived in Las Cruces in August during one of those days of heavy rain at the end of August 2006.

## 5.1  Beginning

I will start with a reconstruction of the history of the bank given by one of the interviewees:

Let's start at the beginning, this bank was chartered in 1905 and that was even before we were a state; the second, and before you leave you need to go up on the wall and look at all the presidents, there are pictures on the wall and the dates are up there, so if I tell you, if I miss something you go up there and verify, I think the second president of the bank was Galles and if have been here long you have heard about Lee Galles, in Albuquerque, Lee Galles, Chrysler, Chevrolet, Cadillac, all that stuff, well their grandfather was the second president of this bank; the third or the fourth president of this bank was a man named Snow, he owned all the farm you know where Stahmann Farms is on Snow Road, and he was known as the "Alfalfa king" and it's all in that book ... [Metz, 1991] he was president for many years; my first recollection of the president was Mr Kelso, he was the longest running president of anybody, he was in the title company business here and I knew him for working in the bank and taking paper work on loans over to him and getting filed and put them together and they didn't write title insurances in those days, they wrote big loan scripts just describing the history of the property and guaranteeing that he didn't have or she didn't have a lain at the bank ... abstract I think they call them (A1).

In this first story extract, we find a brief sketch of the origins of the bank. A first consideration must be made: conversational storytelling is much more fragmented and imprecise than other forms of storytelling, stories that spontaneously emerge in conversations are the result of both consolidated narratives and emergent and contingent reconstruction. What we witness here are strong ties to personal and collective experience, names are connected to places that are part of collective memory, the "alfalfa king" refers to the fact that Oscar Snow had exceptional harvests with alfalfa, one of the most important forage crops in the US agriculture, which he cut four or five times per years. After the first presidents the recollection jumps to personal experience, with Mr Kelso being the first president the interviewee remembers. The short description of this man's work confirms the personal character of the story. There is something mythical about the expression "he was the longest running president of anybody" as well as the sentence "and it was always known as First National Bank of Las Cruces", which also reconnects personal memories with collective memories:

> And it was known always as First National Bank of Las Cruces…and I tell you my family history and you can count or discount that's up to you…my uncle came here in '39 and bought into the Weisenhorn Insurance Company, he was an insurance guy and my dad came here in 1940 to work for him and Mr Papen stayed in the insurance business for…he got married in 1942 his wife was a trouble shooter…her family was involved in the Coca Cola business so she came because this plant was having trouble in Las Cruces, she came here as a trouble shooter to get the plant up and running, and Mr Papen met her and they got together and in about a year they got married, they got married in 1942 and Mr Weisenhorn died about 1950 or 51 and Mr Papen had already bought the insurance company and Mr Weisenhorn was just kind of you know, part of the deal and when he died Mrs Weisenhorn came in and said look Frank my husband has this stock in the bank and he wants you to have it, and he said "stock in the bank? I don't even know"…and so she sold Mr Weisenhorn stock in the bank and he went down to the bank and got it converted to his name (A1).

Here is an example of the difference between conversational, spontaneous storytelling compared to written and thoughtful storytelling (Metz, 1991).

Strong and magnetic individuals have guided the bank since its creation. Nicolas Galles, Oscar Snow, H.B. Holt and William Sutherland are four of many who gave it direction and good judgment during its formative years. Frank O. Papen and a host of others have since guided it to even more impressive heights.

(Metz, 1991, p. xi)

And here is a reconstruction made in an article for the celebration of the ninetieth anniversary:

It started as a dream by a handful of local business leaders who saw the potential for a great future in a small community on the banks of the Rio Grande in southern New Mexico ... the history of the institution is as fascinating as the region it serves. Its growth and development was the reflection of the contributions it made to the economic engine that has today made Las Cruces and Dona Ana County one of the fastest growing regions in the nation ...

In 1951, an energetic young local businessmen who had come to Las Cruces to sell insurance in the early 1940s, acquired his first shares of stock in First National Bank. That man was Frank O. Papen, the man who has guided First National for nearly half of its years in existence to become the dynamic institution that it is today.

In conversational storytelling stories tend to be more fragmented and to intertwine with personal experience. Written storytelling is thoughtful reconstruction and tends to eliminate incongruence and digressions. Conversational storytelling spontaneously evoked is more lively, it is in the flow of experience. I will come back to such argument in the seventh chapter.

At this level we can already notice that the stories arising from conversational storytelling are always personal organizations of experience where the relevant events chosen and the plot may take unlimited configurations.

## 5.2   Frank Papen

Frank is present in the storytelling of each of the interviewees, both the former First National Bank group and the new Wells Fargo group.

There are no doubts that Frank is a myth: he has embodied the bank until his death. As most of the myths, it has been stabilized over the years to expunge that irrational power which is the fabric of every myth. Frank had to break away from the past at his time, he was the new, and he basically had to overthrow the consolidated order.

Here is an interesting extract from one of the interviews:

> They put him on the board in about 1954 and Mr Papen was that kind of guy that was always in charge...he did not have a lot of patience if you do want to do his way fine but he was going to do his business his own way (A1).

There is a dialectic they/him in this sentence "they" refers to the old guard, safe, conservative, nonprogressive members of the board, it is interesting noticing from a storytelling point of view that this sentence "they put him on the board and he was..." has a very different pattern than "they put him on the board because" and this is the very nature of storytelling, it is not rational argumentation it is just the telling to somebody else that something happened, where connections are multiple and even conflicting, as in this case. What is possible in conversational storytelling is more difficult to achieve in the written text, where articulation is less spontaneous. Here is a more rational explanation:

> First National Bank of Las Cruces had become a very safe, conservative bank. Kelso, Aragon and the others managed it honestly and carefully, but cautious, honest management was not the issue with board members represented by Papen. The issue was being overly conservative...Part of the explanation lies in the Great Depression and World War II. Bankers of the 1940s and fifties perceived their colleagues prior to the 1930s as "wheeler-dealers", dreamers and visionaries, gamblers first one scheme after the other, men never satisfied with the status quo. Those risk takers has crashed during the early 1930s...and if any lesson emerged, it was that bankers should avoid speculation when the potential for failure existed...Meanwhile Las Cruces had expanded into a town of 30,000 people who substantially bought their entertainment, their

shoes, shirts, medical care and groceries at El Paso, forty-five miles south. Farmers and businessmen borrowed from El Paso banks.

(Metz, p. 113)

We learn from the interviews that this is exactly what Papen will fight against by bringing businesses, building mall facilities and contributing to the growth of the town.

I will return later to these aspects when talking about Frank's involvement with the community. Here I just wanted to show how conversational storytelling witnesses this initial dialectic of the novelty Frank represented.

Of course Frank was not alone:

Mr Valdes he was the Ford dealer here … and a guy names Claude Tharp who owned the Roundtree Cotton Company here and at that time cotton was the big thing here, always cotton and agriculture was the big thing here and he was also board of the first Baptist Church and Mr Valdes was in charge of the Catholic church, so he had the Hispanic and the Catholics and the Baptists, the farmers, so he tried to cover all the basis with the bank (A1).

Here is the description given by Metz:

Leo Valdes was president of the Mesilla Motor Company, a director of the Rocky Mountain Ford Dealers Advertising Association … Valdes had been born in Chihuahua, but at the age of three his parents migrated to Ysleta in 1910 as a result of the pending Mexican Revolution. His father operated a movie theater for a short time, and then moved to Las Cruces. Valdes graduated from school and began selling cars in 1937. He served one term as a state representative, and a brief time as country commissioner and school superintendent. He resigned everything to serve in the Navy during World War II. People respected the soft-spoken Valdes … Tharp was noncontroversial. The community respected him. Tharp was honest, loyal and had a legion of friends among Mesilla Valley cotton farmers.

(Metz, pp. 115–116)

There is a legitimation issue expressed in these lines that we cannot fully understand if we don't know this story:

> It began with a Sunday meeting in November 1957 at the residence of Frank Papen in Las Cruces. All board members except President Jake Aragon were invited but not knowing this, Glenn Hamill passed Jake's house, saw him watering the lawn and stopped to say, "Jake, how come you aren't over at Frank's?" Aragon said he didn't know anything about the gathering. A somewhat flustered Hamill then continued on, later learning that while the meeting wasn't exactly about Aragon, it was about how the bank might be guided in a more enterprising fashion. And Aragon was perceived as a primary obstacle. After the meeting ended, Aragon went to Papen's house and demanded explanation. A dispute arose and Aragon resigned. The Farmers and Merchant Bank hired him immediately.
>
> (From an interview of Metz with Frank Papen, 11 May 1988)

Here a the reconstruction from one of the interviewees:

> I went to work for him [Frank Papen] in May and in June he already got in Charles Haner who was a bank examiner to come in and run the bank for him and then he fired the president of the bank there is his picture up there up on the wall I will show you where all that is, his name was Jake Aragon (A1).

Here we find a classical example of what Boje talks about in his 1991 article when defining glossing over ambiguity.

Here is how Haner entered in the bank in the words of Leon Metz:

> In 1956, Haner encountered Frank Papen during his [Haner's] periodic bank inspections. Papen strolled over from the insurance office and hung around all day, questioning Haner about banking practices. For several weeks in 1957, after Haner returned to Lubbock on Friday, on Saturday Papen would call, saying he was in town. So the two met for dinner or coffee. During the second examination in 1957, Frank Papen offered Charles Haner a position as a vice president and cashier.
>
> (Metz, p. 118)

We will find this informal meeting procedure also in the recollections of the three executives interviewed.

And here is the reconstruction of the entering of Haner by another interviewee:

> The guy that was president of this bank from about 1969/1970 until early nineties when I took over the job, Frank was president during that time, the guy that was president of the bank at that time was a guy named Charles Haner and Charles was former bank examiner and he was basically self thought because he had high school education but he had no college and he was a product of his time, he started working in the bank when he was 17 or 18 years old and then he went to work for the Office of the Comptroller of the Currency which are the regulators for national banks and at that time they did not require a college education, they just required some experience and he…and he ended up head examiner and he used to examine this bank when he was head examiner and because of the problems that they were having and Frank Papen, who owned the management control of the bank, he hired Charles to come in and straighten that out and so a lot of the thing that transpire during that time that Charles come to work until he got sick and he was involved in a car accident and had a tragic end, really, but he is the guy that I really credit for having saved the bank a couple of times in that process because Frank was not a banker, and the book says it and also John probably would have told you that (C1).

The fact that Frank was not a banker is one expressed by almost all the people we interviewed, they all credited him for being a people person, for having transformed the community of Las Cruces and modernized the town, but the "Frank was not a banker" is a kind of a constant refrain, in the organizational storytelling I have witnessed.

Here are some examples of this refrain in both written and conversational storytelling.

> Frank Papen was not a banker. He didn't know banking laws and banking procedures. He was an insurance man and he knew insurance backwards and forwards. That's why he asked me to come in.

> He knew how to pick good people who knew banking, and therein lies his success.
>
> (Haner interview with Metz, 6 June 1989)

And one of the interviewees:

> In a lot of respect the executive vice-president does much more management than the president does, in some instance I know that was true when Frank Papen was the president and Charles was the executive vice-president, lot of people consider this sacrilegious to say about Frank Papen, but he was not a banker...he was a people person, he understood people and he just had the ability to gain people respect and confidence and I don't think he ever mistrusted anybody, oh that's extreme I am sure he did but he liked people (B1).

Another interviewee:

> He was an external kind a guy and he was a product of his time, and that was the time when you know the sixties and the seventies until you know we went through that first wave of energy that first oil embargo 72–73 United States has a sort of predictor projections in terms of economics after the second world war we weren't having some of those wild kind of swings in the economy...so his old job was selling and he would, I don't know if it says anything in the book about it, but he would have admitted himself he would go down to the lower valley which was where he was from, the Anthony area and would sell loans to people, he would go and talk to this guy and collateral was not an issue to him, he just knew them, he knew that they were good old boys and Charles was the guy that had to manage all that because he knew the safety and soundness issues and Frank was an insurance agent and he sold insurances and he sold bank services in the way he sold insurances (C1).

It must be noticed here that there are a lot of historical references in the excerpt that are edited in this chapter. Some of them are references to US history, some to the local history; some refer to the historical development of banking and community banking in the United States. Although this chapter and the book in general do not seek to be a recollection of US banking history, this is a frame that cannot be neglected. Some of the turns of historical developments have become part of the social history such as the stock market crash in 1929, rather than the Great Depression or World War II, or again the economic slows of the eighties. Some other aspects such as the McFadden Act of 1927, which prohibited interstate bank branching in the United States, and the 1994 Riegle-Neal Act, which eliminated barriers to full interstate banking, represent the institutional background and are inscribed in a broader social history of the United States to which this study could refer.

Historical changes of the working industries have fostered sociological inquiries such as that of Richard Sennett (1998). In this case also the social history is the landscape in which the sociological articulation is inscribed rather than its focus.

Sociologist work is not that of historians, although some of the oral historian sensitivity may be closer to that of sociological work using narrative interviews like mine. What needs to be said is that beside the fact that oral historians need to be more precise about the proof of legitimacy of their sources, they tend to be interested in working classes that have no other way to express themselves, rather than dominant classes.

Returning to the storytelling, along with the refrain of "Frank was not a banker" there are a number of stories that are shared by almost all the people interviewed, even the ones that did not belong directly to the bank, one of them is the "Anthony Story".

> One of the most interesting stories that I like to tell, I grew up in the South Valley, and I worked in Anthony, well originally when Mr Papen was putting his bank together the bank was on one side of the street and it was called First State Bank of Anthony, Texas and he bought that bank and changed the name on it to the First National Bank of Anthony and he built a huge beautiful building but what he didn't realized is that he got across the state line . . . Mr Haner and Mr Papen spent considerable time in Washington and they had them to change into First National Bank of Anthony, New Mexico and he changed to the First National Bank of Dona Ana county . . . HE WAS THE ONLY ONE TO EVER MOVE A BANK ACROSS THE STATE LINE AND CHANGE THE NAME OF THE BANK FIVE TIMES (A1).

Here is the same story from different interviewees, it must be noted that it is spontaneous storytelling, I did not ask for a recollection of the particular story: some extracts like this one are in the form of a conversation with my name here (Linda) or sometime (Boje), later on.

(B1): John can tell you the story better and I don't know whether he did it or not, but he [Frank] acquired what was called First National Bank of Anthony, Texas.
(Linda): and he moved it across the state line …
(B1): Right and nobody know by this day how he got that done.
(Linda): and that was something he was really proud of …
(B1): I don't know whether it was a matter of power or he just confused the hell out of people and ended up with what he wanted ((LAUGHS)) I don't know, but he was able to get things done, his attitude was if it need to be done we will find a way to get it done and that was his ( ) to go head and try.

Another account by a different interviewee:

Because when he bought that bank in Anthony, went down on a weekend talked with somebody in the bank and he got his buddy to build, they found some land and got his buddy to give a favorable bid on building that building and so they had the building built the way I remember the story I don't know if I am totally accurate on this, the way I remember the building was built and it suddenly occurred that the bank was not in New Mexico was in Texas and had to be moved and those days they had the ban on interstate banking, and so after several trips to Washington he and Charles Haner the guy I was talking about, Charles primarily because Charles knew all the players in Washington and he was a good friend of the Comptroller of the Currency at that time and they went back on several occasions and finally closed one eye and keep reading the statute and keep rereading them and finally found that there was a comma left out of one sentences that changed the meaning of a sentence, that allowed that bank to move over to the New Mexico, so they gave the approval and then they went back and cleaned the act and that's a true story and that would never happen today either (C1).

Frank's stories are part of the collective memory of the community of bankers interviewed; when we talk about the tower or the pictures on the walls of the bank we are also relating to collective memory. There are a number of sociological works on collective memory, among the others the work of Maurice Halbwachs (1980) has made it clear how collective memory is social construction activated by each and every community in a constant process of selection and reconstruction of significant events. What is interesting for this work is the idea that the past is reconstructed from the present following different and alternative paths according to the different groups by which they are activated. Namer (1987) argues that collective memory reconstruction happens through the discursive interaction among the members of different social groups.

In one of the brochures we found at Wells Fargo bank there is an historical recollection of the presence of Wells Fargo in New Mexico. The title of the brochure is *Wells Fargo in New Mexico – The legend continues*, making a connection between the services provided to western pioneers by Wells Fargo agents in Albuquerque, Santa Fe and Las Cruces.

> Wells Fargo agents in Albuquerque, Santa Fe and Las Cruces and more than a hundred other New Mexico towns delivered convenient, reliable service that Wells Fargo customers enjoyed then, and can still expect today (Wells Fargo brochure).

What is interesting is that Wells Fargo bank, the way it is now, is the result of an incredible number of mergers to the point that it can hardly be identified with the company described in the brochure shown in Figure 5.2.

What is also peculiar is that in the account provided in the brochure First National Bank disappears from history:

> In 1998, Wells Fargo and Norwest joined in a merger of equals. Then at the beginning of this new century, Wells Fargo acquired First National Bank of Farmington and First Security offices in the greater metropolitan area of Albuquerque, Las Cruces, Roswell and Santa Fe. The heritage of these pioneer New Mexico financial institutions lives under the familiar Wells Fargo name.

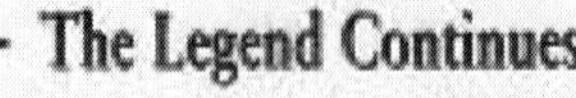

*Figure 5.2*   Brochure of Wells Fargo Bank.

What survives in the orality is neglected in the textuality. Returning to the orality, Frank Papen is described as a man of a different time:

> Those days Las Cruces was very small he was shaking everybody's hands and you are banking with me and that's how he built up the bank (A1).

The sense of responsibility not only for his bank but also for his own community is a distinctive trait of his personality:

> (Boje):  you are talking about risk and reward, was your uncle a risk taker, how would he fit in there?
>
> (A1):  His philosophy was so different, he wanted to do what was best for the community, if that took risk then … you see across the street there is a mall, that was the first enclosed mall between Dallas and Phoenix in 1964 and he built that mall so that people like you from the University would stay here and spend their money rather than go to El Paso, he didn't build that mall with the idea of making money, he built that shopping center to keep people in Las Cruces to spend their money and he built streets and roads and he would go to the University when Dr Corbett was president and if he would see somebody's car with a sticker from El Paso he would say how could he bought the car in El Paso? We need him to buy locally, he never thought about risk and reward rather than we would be sitting across the table from him and talk about the loans and this is the risk and this is the reward and what do we want to do and he would say you are the experts, you take care of that.

And here another interviewee:

> Well, I can tell you that the modern day banker version of community involvement in not the same of the community involvement activities of people that came out of Frank's generation because they were involved in everything and up to their neck and they could spend, a guy in Frank's job, if he never came in to the bank it wouldn't have made any difference, he was out involved in the chambers of commerce, he was involved with economic development and all these other issue and to an extend I got involved in some of those that I didn't spend a lot time in because I was involved in risk management issues, and that clears the difference, a guy in Jim's job today his performance is measured on internal numbers, it's not in his memberships, so his orientation is completely different, he has a commitment in the community but it's a different kind of commitment (C1).

Here the reference is to people that occupy the highest position for the southern New Mexico area within the Wells Fargo bank compared to the old community bank positions. We will see that this is a recurrent theme in the next sections.

Returning to Frank, part of his involvement was bringing business to the community:

> ((Looking at the pictures on the shelves)) He looked for a site to put a plant...and Mr Papen you need a little help, you need to move here in Las Cruces and they spurred a little while and they canceled the guys plane and they brought him up here and put him up at his house and showed him around town (A1).

"They" probably refers to the Amigos, an old New Mexico group to which Papen did belong.

> (A1):  Well, they put the plant down in Mesilla Park and they guaranteed him that they had 75 employees when they got up and running and at its peak they had 1300 people working there.
>
> (Boje):  13 hundred?
>
> (A1):  Yes ((PAUSE)) and it's now shut down...
>
> (Boje):  when did it shot down?
>
> (A1):  Let's see what are we now? 2006? Probably it was 1992 or 1993 Stan Smith he was one of our directors he was a manager of the plant when they shot it down ((PAUSE)) they couldn't make it... ...but for the years they made it! ((Expression of the face))...then you know...when the market changed...so they shot that thing down and now belongs to a lumber company or something I don't know...yeah...well that was one of the many things that Mr Papen brought to Las Cruces.

We can see in this short conversational extract two poles of narration, on the one hand the pole of social recounting, where the bringing of business by Papen is reconstructed along with the success of the company and the second pole is that of experience, of the reinscription of personal experience and personal meaning to the abovementioned narrative. It is a different time and different place, also expressed in the different tone of the voice and the facial expression: the sentence "and it's now shut down" tells us more than a temporal event, offers us an opening to a dialectic that, despite an attempt to rationalize in the following sentence, "the market changed", remains at that level as a rough material.

The last sentence, "well that was one of the many things that Mr Papen brought to Las Cruces" brings back to the socialized "we" and reconnects in the following sentence to the "I", through "he was my uncle".

(Boje):  Mr Papen...
(A1):  He was my uncle, he bought this bank in 1957 and I went to work for him in May 1958.

Here is another story of Papen bringing business to the community:

(A1):  People just don't know what Mr Papen did, have you ever been to Berino, New Mexico?
(Boje):  no, but we can go there.
(A1):  On the way to El Paso you know where the police station is on the left hand side if you look over to the right side you see a huge building, you know what that is? It is the McNary eggs, they produce all the local eggs that are sold in the stores, if you go to Alberston it says McNary egg somewhere, well Mr Papen got them here and it's a huge company and they hire a lot of people... it's a huge deal and nobody even relates those kind of things to what he did... like he brought the Hanes company down.

There is a sense of continuity in the sentence "if you go to Alberston": Alberston is one of the supermarkets you can find in Las Cruces and the one where I shopped during my stay. I actually checked when got back home and found that I had bought, without knowing, eggs that were produced by that company.

Frank contributed to the building of a number of facilities, the tower in the first place:

In around late 1964–1965 the year after Mr Papen built the Loretto shopping center across the street from the bank, which is this one back over there, he was talking with our two senators in Washington, Clinton Anderson and senator Dennis Chavez and they were talking … the government was trying to put a NASA site in California or Florida and the New Mexico delegation wanted to bring it to New Mexico at White Sands Missile Range, because of the weather and the timing and so Mr Papen went back to Washington to encouraged them to bring the NASA site to Las Cruces and White Sands, the major objective that he was told was that there was no office space in Las Cruces for them to office in, so they really couldn't come to Las Cruces and started to formulate an idea of building a building to house them, his original intention was to build a seven story building to house the bank on the ground floor and the upper floors to be for NASA and so he started on that project and the building project started in 1966 late '66 and ended in '67. Every week or every two week Mr Papen would call our delegation asking where the NASA people were and they couldn't get it through Congress to bring the NASA facilities to White Sands, in the meanwhile he finished the building and moved offices of the branches, the Installment Loan Department moved into the building and he moved the stockbrokers in there and the telephone company, the hole rest of the building was empty, he had increased the size, the contractors convinced him to increase the size of the bank from seven story to ten story and for about two and a half years the building was completely empty and Mr Papen called every month wondering where NASA was, well the Government did approve, the Congress did approve the NASA site Johnson Space Center which is now here in White Sands … he finally rent the building and that was a very prestigious address for many many years for people, some of these people have been in the building, one firm in particular from the very beginning, it was our accountants, it's on the tenth floor (A1).

There are a lot of stories around the tower and what is fascinating is that four out of five people interviewed spontaneously told us stories about the construction of it, we can easily affirm that the tower it is not only a feature of Las Cruces landscape but its story is actually part of the collective memory of this community and survives in the orality.

Here is one of the interviewees' accounts:

((Leafing through the book)) There's our tower. There's the tower downtown here, now the Wells Fargo tower, built in 1967. My understanding is that when they built the building it was going to be seven storey high and then Frank Papen was having a cocktail with the contractor and said what would it take to go up another three, so all the utilities, all that is on the seventh floor, where typically would be up on top, they had three more floors, that's what Ben and John have told me, the old facts (D2).

Another interviewee:

And originally was going to be a seven story, well he wanted a ten story building and they couldn't make its feasibility work and so they finally settle to seven and as a side the economy was in a tank in the late sixties and they guy that was building it had another job that fell through and he had a bunch of crew that he needed to keep busy so he went to Frank and said I'll put the other three story of that building for 300,000 I don't remember the number but significantly less it would have been had we contracted before because he was trying to keep his crew busy, so that's how it ended up to be a ten story building, if you go downtown and you go through that building today you would see that the air conditioning and all the mechanical is on the seventh floor and that's why, because it was already been topped out when they came to it (C1).

These excerpts provide an example of terse storytelling as defined by Boje in 1991, and recollected in Chapter 2, in particular they show us the dynamic aspect of terse storytelling where each members decides to accentuate certain aspects over others.

What is interesting is that Frank's figure is equally recognized by the people that served at the bank but also by those that were part of the acquiring team (the second acquiring team, as we did not interview the first acquiring team, although there are a lot of references to them in the "Acquisitions" section of this chapter).

I did meet him [Frank] just the patriarch at the bank there, he was a state senator and just WELL, WELL REGARDED (D2).

*Figure 5.3*   Papen Memorial. (Picture taken by Marisa Ortman.)

There is a Frank Papen memorial in front of the bank located between Main Street and Lohman Ave, shown in Figure 5.3.

The figure of Frank Papen haunts the tower of the bank and the lobby where you can see the murals that he commissioned, by Manuel Acosta, in 1962.

> Papen talked to Manuel Acosta, explaining that the bank wanted a history of the Mesilla Valley in pictorial form.
>
> (Metz, 1991, p. 137)

It is a rather naive rendition of the history of the Mesilla Valley:

> The murals opened with a conquistador standing beside a captured Apache. (The conquistador was Javier Adalto who worked for State Farm in El Paso. Eduardo Gonzalez was the Indian.) The second panel continued the Indian conquest. It featured a Franciscan father imploring both side to accept God and peace…A valiant pioneer lady posed with her children. (Betty Armstrong of the

Mesilla Book Store was the model) The next panel described the Wild West … the mural progression then moved on to Fort Selden, a (genuine) Loretto nun, an adobero constructing a typical New Mexico residence, a santero carving a wooden Santo, an early railroad engine, the Loretto Academy and a typical home of the period. (Manuel Acosta was the santero. Lucas Herrera of Radio Shack was the man with the mule. Nina Maria Jemente was the young girl reading. The boy sitting alongside was Frank O. Papen jr., who would die tragically shortly afterwards when an automobile struck him). A typical vaquero represented the transition into modern times (Daniel Herrera, brother to Lucas, stood tall in a blue shirt, black hat and rope). "I painted him alone on a panel because he brought all this remarkable equipment, including the chaps, from Marfa, Texas" Acosta said. "The gear was magnificent". The last horizontal scene placed Dona Ana County in the modern world. Mariachis played in front of the First National Bank building. Geese waddled among the pecan trees at Stahmann Farms. The administration building appeared at New Mexico State University. A missile represented White Sands, cotton the farmers, and a dam for Elephant Butte.

(Metz, 1991, pp. 137–138)

The murals represent an extraordinary visual expression of collective memory of the community. As we have seen, the stories of Frank are part of the collective memory of the bankers but there are also a number of artifacts to which such collective memory refers: they are for example the Papen's memorial in front of the bank, the pictures of the presidents in the bank's lobby, and the tower itself.

## 5.3   Life at first national bank

The recollections of life at First National bank are the recollection of a golden age, the climate seems to reflect the external pleasant and stable weather of the south west. Although some recollected the terrible floods during the summer, showing how people experience reality in different ways, deciding upon which aspect to give emphasis to and which aspects to gloss over.

Here is what said one of the interviewees:

> We wanted a good life and it's a good life here, we had a good time and Mr Papen loved to shake hands and hug people and tell them how good they were doing and how wonderful everything was, you know he was just that kind of guy (A1).

Here is an extract from a newsletter of the bank for the employees of 1980:

> At a recent stockholder meeting, our Chairman of the Board, State Sen. Frank O. Papen, spoke on the history of First National Bank since its founding in 1905 with only $25,000 worth of capital. After reviewing the past however senator Papen turned his remarks to the future and the decade of the 1980s, noting "The next decade will be a period of even greater growth for New Mexico than ever before. Our climate, our natural resources and the incredible variety of recreational opportunities in our state will guarantee our economic well being almost in spite of what may happen at a national level."
>
> (Vol. VII, No. 5, April 1980)

And again another extract from the same year:

> Everything is changing so fast. Prices seem to leap upward. Word politics are unstable. Pollution keeps gnawing holes in the ecology. We worry more and relax less. But some things don't change. The strength and reliability of our bank, the First National Bank of Dona Ana County, proves it.
>
> (Vol. VII, No. 5, April 1980)

The themes of safety and continuity become recurrent in both the organizational storytelling and in its symbols:

> Our symbol was just a circle and then we put the name in it and our theme was "we are here for you today and we will be here for you tomorrow" and a jingle and they had that for 25 years (A1).

Says one of the interviewees.

> When I browsed the newsletters I found an entire world: letters of
> appreciation from the customers; reward prizes for the employees;
> Christmas party pictures; social events like the First National Bank
> hot air balloon ... and I really had an hard time not to believe that
> that was a golden age in which Mr Papen was some kind of a royal
> figure. Mr Papen considered every employee here part of his fam-
> ily, it was all a family atmosphere, everybody got along to a certain
> degree ... and it's just like marriages, you don't go along with your
> husband all the time, but in the end you are fine and so that's the
> way they ran the bank all those years, and everybody loved Mr
> Papen, I don't know anybody who didn't love Mr Papen, he was
> an icon (A1).

And again from the same interviewee:

> People were proud to be part of the bank, it was a unique bank,
> and we were above everybody here: we always had the first
> products (A1).

And again:

> And did you see our logo everywhere? ((Looking at the newslet-
> ters)) in fact I wore a jacket the other day with our logo ... and the
> pins, I will bring you my pin ... and the song and that jingle, every
> ad we ever ran on the TV or the radio had that jingle, we are here
> for you today and we will be here for you tomorrow, it was some
> pretty awesome time (A1).

From the same interview:

> We have been here hundred years, long time, New Mexico hasn't
> been a state one hundred years, 1912 is when New Mexico became
> a state, so they won't be 100 years until 2012, but we would have
> been 100 years old last year in 2005 if we still would be FNB we
> had a big ... ask about the big party we had for our ninetieth birth-
> day ... and we run a contest for the people that had the oldest

accounts in the bank, with very good prizes and one of my very very good friend told me he was SURE he was going to win the first prize because he had an account here from 1942 the month I was born April 1942 "Papen I am going to win that prize" he said and it went on and on for 60 or 90 days and it turned there were people that banked with us before the Depression and still had their bank accounts from the twenties…we had a big party on the steps we had several hundred people and we gave them sodas and soft drinks and cakes, we had a big cake and I passed out cake to everybody (A1).

Here's an excerpt from the special edition of the newsletter:

As part of its 90th Anniversary, First National Bank of Dona Ana County decided to seek the individual or individuals who had been customers of the bank for the longest period of time…we received more than 300 calls and letters from long-time customers, many of them who have been with us since the 1920s and 1930s.

Not only customers were loyal to the First National, many of the First National Bank employees had been on the job for more than 20 years, and a survey conducted on the ninetieth anniversary showed how the average years of experience at First National per employee was 8.7, which is an extremely high number.

## 5.4   Decision makers

In this section I will include extracts of the accounts of decision makers talking about decision-making processes at both the community bank and at the local level of the Wells Fargo bank and their personal work histories as decision makers.

Here is the recollection of one of the decision makers of the community bank:

In the early days, my early days, one of the big profit maker for the bank was the lending and that's what I did all my life; I was a lender (A1).

This sentence is interesting as it emphasizes the identity dimension of working life, and again:

> The big emphasis was on consumer lending, and I ran the consumer lending for many years, and where we really made our mark was the automobile business from the early sixties, 63, 64 to the mid-eighties we were probably the number one auto financer in Dona Ana County we had all the dealers…we had millions and millions of dollars in car people…and that changed when the manufacturers got in…Anyway that's how we made our money for many and many years (A1).

The final sentence "anyway that's how we made our money…", signals a third time of narrative, between the "we" of the sentences "one of the big profit maker was the lending" and "we really made our mark in the automobile business", and the second time of "and that changed…", the third time is the personal reconstruction that signals clearly where the identity of the interviewee lies.

There are three people talking in this chapter from the former First National bank and they all introduce the others to us in an interesting chiastic structure:

> You may or may not know him, a guy named Tom Mobley and he was our trust officer for 30 and plus years and in the trust department he also handled the bank investment portfolio and he did all the investing for the bank as far as loans and treasury bills (A1).

"You may or you may not know" signals a way of talking that expresses being rooted in a community and a strong orality dimension.

Here is how the bankers introduce themselves and their role in the bank as decision makers:

> (Linda): in another interview you said you, Tom and Ben made the big decisions (A1): originally it was Mr Papen and Mr Haner, Tom Mobley, Ben Haines and myself, and then as the bank grew we brought other people in…but basically the bank was really run by Ben Haines who was number one guy and Tom and I were the number two guys.

And from another interviewee:

> Well, John was really number two and I was probably number three. I actually…when I went working for the bank I was hired as an agricultural loan officer I started February 1970 and for the balance of that year that was my job, to head the agricultural lending program…at the end of 1970 Frank Papen had become so involved in the political activities of the state actually being the state senator and he was spending more and more time in Santa Fe and so he, well officially the board, Frank, so basically the board, the board decisions was always Frank decisions, but anyway he appointed Charles as president of the bank and Charles asked me to be in charge of the lending function of the bank and I stayed in that position for two years and during that time John was in charge of the consumer lending or what we referred as installment lending at that time, so John was reporting to me so it was pretty uncomfortable position to tell you the truth, because he was Frank nephew and very close to him, Frank frequently introduced John as his son…Frank and his wife Julie had two children, Frank junior and Michele was the daughter, older, Frankie was killed in an automobile accident when he was about ten, so I guess John in Frank's mind, I don't think he did consciously, John had replaced Frank in a lot of respect…so I was really uncomfortable acting as I was John boss so when Payne left the bank and they asked me to take with the investment and trust function, John moved into the head of the lending function and it was actually a relief to me ((LAUGHS)) I am not sure what point I was trying to make here, yes you started saying that John and I were number two so John became number two and I became number three (B1).

This long excerpt shows how the account "Ben was number one and John and I were number two" is challenged following an idea of respect for Frank's family.

And yet the other interviewee:

> Well, John was…first of all John and I are closer than most of our family members are to us, we kind of grew up in this thing together and we have seen the good and the bad and the ugly, so we have a bond that has worked well for us a lot of times and a lot of ways,

sometimes has gotten into way but John and I have a very good relationship and from the outside looking in lot of people would be puzzled about that because of the family involvement but we both respected the other strengths and I never wanted to do the things that John was good at and he never wanted to do the things that I was good at and so . . . John is a community person he, there is hardly anybody in town that don't know him, and I guess in some ways is like Ben and Jerry ice cream, when people talk about one they talk about the others, John he is much better known than I am and I couldn't have done what I needed to do If I haven't if I had trying to do his role and he wouldn't have been comfortable doing what I did (C1).

Who continues, talking about John:

I think John doesn't give himself near enough credit for what he is capable of . . . there is nobody who has better recall that John does . . . and he could recount conversation with customers that he had 25 years ago (C1).

And Tom:

Tom of the three of us he is the most analytical of all us, and if you had to ask Tom what time of the day is, before telling you, he would build a watch and I have told him that and I have used his strengths a lot of times because he handled our investment portfolio for . . . I respected his judgment on things and I knew he was never gonna . . . his philosophy is not ready, fire, aim, he . . . he aims first, he is very methodical about it and he goes to the process before he makes the decision and . . . I tend to operate a little bit more on I instinct but our management team was not a one man show but any means and it was our greater strengths and it was our greater weakness because I thought I figured we were all on this thing together, there were four of us in senior management and as far as I was concerned they were all . . . I would make the tough decisions if decision had to be made on something, sometimes they didn't agree with me it wasn't by vote, but if one of them was against something that were going to do, unless it was an imperative I would rethink the process we would talk about it and reach a consensus and it's interesting because our compensation programs a lot of times, people would scratch their head today on it because we didn't differentiate, because I needed those guys, I know I couldn't make without them…we had a strong bond among us, which you don't get today and I don't know if you could afford to do that today especially in an organization that has 170,000 people working like Wells Fargo has got you can't manage that way (C1).

Along with the chiastic structure these conversational storytelling fragments reveal to us a dimension of decision-making that is often time neglected in the organizational textbooks, its social dimension. All three interviewees have introduced the other partners in the managing team of the bank in a very personal and intimate way, friendship, respect and genuine appreciation in these extracts are really self-explaining in this sense.

Here is a more formal question about decision, one of the interviewees mentioned the word "big decisions" and I asked him what that means.

(Linda):  what do you mean by big decisions?

(A1):  All investment decisions: where to put the bank's money; the major loan decisions: who would we loan the big loans to, the multimillion dollar deals; and the operations of it, we made decisions about you know, what we do with our branches, who ran them, our personnel decisions, what we were going to do in Hatch, Santa Teresa, what we wanted to do in White Sands, things like that. So for those big decisions we would sit around a table like this and we made, we ran the bank, we ran the company.

(Linda):  and how was it, I mean the process?

(A1)  It was awesome! A lot of times we disagreed on a lot of things and especially in loans I would want to sell a loan and Ben and Tom would say no, we don't do this and we don't like this, do this and this and this, but we walked out of the door and we were all together we were a team, we never walked out and I never told a loan customer not, we were all a team and everybody sang the same song…and that's the way Mr Papen wanted it…and we did that for 25–30 years in the bank.

Again the social dimension of decision-making processes. It is interesting noticing, compared to formal models of decision-making that I will describe in the last chapter, how the processes are much more fluid, "we would sit around a table like this and we would run the bank, we ran the company". Decisions happen in the everyday life of decision makers and they are tied to their experience, personal values and recognition such as the "and that's the way Mr Papen wanted...".

The decision-making process is sometimes hardly traceable:

> We all knew, when we went to a meeting we knew what we were going to talk about, the one in charge of that particular area carried the conversation and we interacted...we just sat around a table and had a cup of coffee and made the decisions we had to make (A1).

Returning to decision maker's careers and identity at work:

> It's always been kind of a mystery to me how I moved through my banking career because my degree from university was in Agronomy and I worked for a year as a salesman for a seed company in Texas and during that time my wife and I married, she was 18 at the time, we married and never been away from home and we were living in Texas and she got very homesick, her dad had a ranch in the northern part of the county and he needed somebody to run the ranch so I came home to run the ranch for them and in two years ((LAUGHS)) my car was wearing out, my clothes were wearing out, and I was just surviving and I remember reading the Panorama from the university and see classmates who did not have the same degree of success that I have had as a student but I would see these notices and see how they became officers in the military and you see notices as promotion to major...corporate officers and here I was just a...cowboy. So I decided I had to do something that made more sense and as it happened I was offered a job with the federal land bank to make long term mortgage loans of farms and ranches and that was the reason why I was asked to go work for the First National Bank...so my education was not in finance, was not in any of the tradition disciplines that you look for in a bank so all my banking education and knowledge was acquired on the job, I attended seminars, of course I went

to several banking schools that were sponsored by the American Banking Association … all this to say that when I took the trust department I didn't even know what a trust was, I don't even know that I knew what a treasury bill was but ((LAUGHS)) but I remember that Frank and Charles called me into the office and they have been interviewing people for several weeks and I know that they had one candidate that had flown in from Chicago and the only thing I can conclude is that they were never able to reach a salary agreement with that candidate so they called me and at that time the trust department had a lot of trust that were in farm land, I think that was what it was … they knew I had a lot of agricultural knowledge … but I still didn't know what a trust was ((LAUGHS)) … but it was a great experience and I had a lot of support from the staff and the person that was actually second in charge of the department he was very supportive and I was very fortunate to hire some very good people (B1).

Life at the community bank for a decision maker then was quite different than at a large institution such as Wells Fargo today. Here is one of the interviewees talking about procedures:

First National Bank was really just a county bank when I came to work in 1970 there were very very few written policies, I remember very distinctly that the loan application that I was provided was just a white sheet of paper ((laughs)) with the space for the names, the address, date and the amount of loan request everything else was just a white sheet of paper, so that sheet of paper and the promissory note and whatever collateral instrument was the loan file … well we did do, we did get financial statements and we did some analysis of financial statements but there were no written policies so one of my first jobs was to try to develop a policy manual and it was a huge undertaking, in fact I never completed the project and before we got too far into it I moved into the trust department (B1).

And again:

But the level of regulatory control was much lower in those days, I guess the examining function was to take a look at the credit quality and if you didn't have bad loans, look at the liquidity, look at the mandatory reserves that you had to maintain and as long as you were within the limitations that were considered successful by the examiners then everything was okay … I don't really think they went beyond that but that was just the beginning of the time when we started to see more and more bank regulation and so the big difference that existed back then compared to now is that a lot of the management decisions were based on the vision of the individual manager and the actual practice in my view was more a function of what appeared to be prudent and sound based on common sense as opposed to meeting any defined criteria and now I guess all banks also the small community banks are heavily regulated and management just doesn't have the latitude that we once had when I talk about latitude one of the things that comes to my mind is that first thing that every officer in the bank did when he came to work was to look at the reject list, the list of checks that bounced, we called them bounced, they were checks that wouldn't clear the account when they were presented and so the decision that had to be made in the very next day was whether or not you were going to pay them in the overdraft or you were going to return, so you would come to the front door, you would go to a counter where the list laid and before you even took off your coat you would go through the list and you would initials the ones you would go ahead and pay and anything that was not initialed got returned and the decision was just based on … you don't see this kind of things happening anymore (B1).

This excerpt helps us delineate differences between what it meant to be a banker and a decision maker back then and how it has changed compared to the banking institutions we see nowadays. Storytelling helps us to understand how different people construct different interpretations of this: some of the interviewees see the divide being regulation and the changing market conditions and argue that small banks also now perform differently; others see it as the opposition between community banks and nationwide banks.

Here is another account on responsibilities of bankers and judgment in the community bank era:

You know, one of the responsibilities you had, all officers had, if a non customer wanted to cash a check in the bank we cashed him, it was considered to be part of our responsibilities as a bank to cash checks for people, not just checks from our bank but checks from other banks, of course if the check was from our bank the teller could make the decision, they checked the balance and if the money was there they cashed the check and gave him the money, but if it was from another bank particularly from an out of town bank they needed their boss to okay it, so I asked Charles Haner one day, I asked don't you have any guidance? How am I supposed to know whether that check is good or not? What rule are we supposed to follow? And he said, "if you go and okay the check you are damn sure it doesn't bounce" and I said "how do I know that?" he said: "use your judgment!" and that was it. And I found a book, a little pamphlet that somebody had that talked about the risk of cashing checks and when I finished it I thought there is no way on the earth that you can protect yourself, and a lot of time we would call the bank in which the check was drawn and asked them if there were sufficient funds in the account to cover the check and they can tell you yes but that doesn't mean that the money would be there when the check was presented for payment (B1).

Returning to the social aspects of decision-making processes:

I will tell you, one of the traditions that had evolved was that before the bank opened and after we would review the rejected checks, after we finished that, we would go to the coffee shop and there was a lot of just general conversation we talked about things happening in the community, things that were happening in sports and happening in politics but you always ended up to some extends to things that were affecting the bank and that is not to say that we did not have more structured formalized management meetings, but a lot of the conversations, in the coffee shop had to do with banking and a lot of ideas evolved there, decisions that didn't require a lot of analysis so you made there those decisions, a pretty informal process (B1).

There is a sociological function of the coffee shop, as Jedlowski talks about the functions of storytelling this extract signals the communitarian function of communication. What is important here is not the content of the conversation but the fact of establishing a contact. This brings us very close to the "phatic" dimension of communication that Jacobson talks about.

But not all the members were equally comfortable with the "coffee shop" practice:

> See my background has been with the Federal Land bank and it was highly structured and the applications were very detailed and comprehensive and we had policies for everything so … to be honest I was never totally comfortable with the informal management decision-making process but there was more than one time that I felt like we may be wasting time during those sessions at the coffee shop and I had more important things to do so I quit coming, well when I quit coming I found that I was going out of the loop so quickly … so I started to go back to the coffee shop ((laughs)) (B1).

And again the storytelling being ex-post reconstruction adjusts materials into the coherence of a story line such as the one here of the impossibility of maintaining such processes due to a changing environment:

> It worked [referring to the somehow unstructured decision-making process] and one of the reason why it could work was because of the fact that the bank was still pretty small, you knew all your customers, and so a lot of the judgments that you made with respect to those customers were based on the confidence in them as individuals and their ability to perform on their commitments but as the bank grew the size of the loans got bigger and the population of the community was growing so you were getting people you didn't know and it became imperative that it became more structured but none of that happened overnight I think that all of the structure that came into the management of the bank just evolved based on the perceived needs as the bank was growing (B1).

Here a top executive is talking about a personnel decision during an assessment meeting to raise the pay of the employees of the bank:

> But I got a little bit more aggressive one year, I felt that if there was somebody that was not performing at the level … with their

> salary level, they need to work somewhere else and I made that recommendation (B1).

The "but" introduces dialectic between different orientations; on the one side the profitability issue and on the other side the responsibility that Papen felt toward his employees. I think this example is extremely relevant in a work on decision-making procedures as it shows different systems of judgments that can coexist in the same organization, and storytelling performs in this sense a cognitive function.

> And when we were at a meeting for a specific individual that had worked for the bank for some period of time Frank Papen would say "no, that person has been with us for a long time, we should keep that person" (B1).

Referring to Papen:

> He was intensely loyal to people who worked for him and he expected the same loyalty in return (B1).

And again:

> But over the years it became really obvious that our personnel costs were too high and it was having an adverse effect on profitability but the employees were members of Frank's family and if you have been more than ten years you had to screw up big time to get in trouble…the only way you could get fired from this bank was to get caught stealing or insult the boss' family (B1).

Leading to the conclusion:

> Because of Frank's commitment to his employees we got overstuffed and one of the things that the examiners began to look at in measuring the soundness of the bank was profitability (B1).

And again, from another top executive:

> People of Frank's generation, he was loyal to the people that got into the dance, but the survival of the business required some

things that those people couldn't bring to the table and he still had loyalty to them and to be completely frank, Frank had a lot of struggle with that because my job was to make it work and sometimes you have to make some tough decisions that are inconsistent with that loyalty (C1).

There is a difference, as I said before, between the different narrators: not all of them show the same attitude toward the historical development. In the seventh chapter I will emphasize different types of storytelling and focus on the distinction between constructed and socialized narratives and emergent fragments.

Up to now I have shown extracts from the community bank side, here is the description of the difference between the loan committee procedure and the decentralized procedure done by a member of the Wells Fargo bank:

It's almost the same of saying the good old boys, the way of maybe making a loan that kind of stuff, you know back in the days of the First National Bank of Dona Ana, probably First National Bank of Albuquerque, you know who owned that when I was there, you know the Maloof right, the Palms in Las Vegas, that's them, they were the owners it was George Maloof the father that bought it but when you see those young boys, I used to be on the board of director loan committee they would male loan decision back then but again going back to the independent days of the bank you would have loan committee get together, but it was pretty "hey we are going to do this loan" and it was already pretty much decided that this is the deal that we were going to do and it was a lot of one page type of write-ups, now is very much, you are going to analyze the financials, you are going to do a lot of due diligence, you are going to a lot of things, whereas these were we know the folks we have been in the community long time, yes we got the financials…we are going to still make the deal…they made a lot of money back in those days because that does work, you can't do it these days but it did work back then, you look at a John Papen he knows everybody and that was a big part of it, hey this guy is okay…it was a different way of doing things and you would have a board of directors loan committee for loans over a certain dollar amount, that was just part of their structure saying okay we got to cut off anything over a million dollars we have to bring it to the loan committee the board of directors loan committee that met once a month and they just ratified pretty much the loans, these are the loans that we did and stamp it back on those days those boards directors that were on the independent banks they were actually legal board members (D2).

While nowadays the boards:

Nowadays you hear about our board is an advisory board, they have no legal obligation is just a kind of what's going on in the community, you guys make sure you get us some referral, we'll tell you what's going on in the bank and things like that, so it's a lot different, in a legal board you are actually liable for what the bank has going on, a lot of those banks boards where the bank would go they would go after those board of directors, in those days, they were legal boards, most of the boards now, we still have a legal board at the big Wells Fargo level, but for the local level here we have a board but it's an advisory board and a lot of our board is still members that used to be the legal member of the First National Bank of Dona Aria, and so they have been in the community long time, know a lot of folks (D2).

I think this extract is self-explanatory of this major shift in making decisions for people belonging to a local bank and people being part of a big group where Las Cruces and southern New Mexico is just a little part of it.

You know we are not a loan committee structure, we are more serial approval, the banker approves then it goes to the next up, the next up, it's not that we all get together in a loan committee and everybody is looking at a loan request at one time, back in these days you had a loan committee, they had a meeting probably every week but if you needed to get a deal done before that you probably could, but you had your loan committee and that was typically the day you had all the presentations ready to go and they were presented (D2).

As said before, narrative research helps us to understand how people make sense of situations and institutions in which they live; here is another banker from Wells Fargo:

> You know one of the things that we have to do as a nationwide company is we have to be uniform in our decision-making so, with regard to the regulators I mean if they came in and they will say down there in Las Cruces, Mike is making loans to people who have, you know one of the measurement we are using in lending is debt income, so if I make for every thousand dollar that I make, we say it's okay to have, you can say it's okay to have about four hundred dollars of that amount, maybe 350 dollars in debt payments, if you get much higher than that we say, it's too much strained and we just think that there is too much strain on you, well so that's a 35 per cent debt income ratio well, what if somebody went into a Wells Fargo in Montana and you know we will tolerate a 70 per cent of debt income ratio, the OCC, says, no, wait a minute, you have to apply unified standards across all your banks so that's a lot of the reason that we have centralized underwriting and need to conform to our decision-making processes across our company because, number one provides value as a franchise, number two we have some regulatory concerns about that (E2).

Loan committee procedures are replaced by centralized procedures and thus also the orientation of the job has changed:

> We all have what we call our lending limits, the thing about a larger bank and that's true for and probably for Bank of America and Citibank, we do have a dollar threshold where we have central areas that underwrite, and it makes it much more efficient, because you know from a Wells Fargo standpoint ideally where do we want out business bankers? Out of the bank, calling our customers, calling on prospects, so what we have come up with and it's great, we find a new loan request, we put all the information together, we sent to a central underwriting they are totally geared staffed just to make the write-ups and get the decisions to us so that the bankers are not sitting at the computer, they are out funding new businesses to be able to send, now we still have the ability, if we say that's a deal we still like we can reverse it and go ahead and get it

approved and we have different ways of getting that done, we find the deal, the package then goes to our central underwriter, they do all the work of getting the financial statement spread, doing the credit investigation all of that stuff, so that our bankers can go out and the next day instead of working on your write-up they are talking to the other business owner about a new loan and let's say that they came back and say we don't, we recommend that we do not do this deal, we then can say we like it, we have the ability to overwrite, based on certain thresholds (D2).

And again:

They do a tremendous job they have been business bankers, they have had customers, they know the process, they are very good, we get a two day turnaround time, now that's the max, sometimes it will come back the same day, this deal is slam dunk, let's do it, as opposed to the banker, oh I have got to get this spread, I have to go and do this credit investigations, boy my manager wants me to be out and make more calls but I have to work this, ah men, it's tremendous, it really does work well, Wells Fargo has really done a lot of investment, lot of work to put these centers to where they are very much ... and guess who their customers are, those underwriters, we are, and they realized that we are their customers, the bankers, in all these markets, and guess what, it's all a team approach with the goal of making that customer better off financially, the business, that's our vision ..., it works very well ... but let's say we don't like what they come back, they might approve it, but let's say we need to do it only for three years, we want to do it five, I can say we are going to do a reversal, let's do it for five years (D2).

About the role of the bankers in this context:

What Wells Fargo has said is let's make our bankers be out there, let's give them the ability to be out there making more calls, being out there visiting with their customers, really being ... guess what we call our bankers business relationship managers, we want them to be with the customer not just talking about loans, how about your investments, about your home mortgage, about all the things that we can do and they are the one contact they are the business relationship managers, you know credit is one piece of it, making a loan is one piece of it and we are a financial services provider, we do loan, but we do eighty other things too (D2).

This passage shows us very well the selling orientation of the bank, also the vocabulary "business relationship managers" is part of this culture; we will hear other terms belonging to this selling culture such as the branches being called "stores". We will see that this comes from the Norwest culture and in particular from the CEO, Dick Kovacevich.
   On the selling culture:

It's the hunter and the gatherers, they go out and get it, I am going to be the analyst the underwriting guy that skins it and tears it apart; men we got a deal here, but guess what, stay out there and go find me more (D2).

And again:

We want our bankers out so that while they have a half a million dollar deal working hopefully they are out the next day to get another one, send it in and we are getting more and more on the books (D2).

Bankers of Wells Fargo have worked for small community banks as well and thus recognize the differences:

As I said I worked for the National Bank of Belen for about five years and we had a loan committee and you would sign off on a loan as a group, now it's here's our policy if it fits with it it's signed off if it deviates we have to document and give the reason why but it's a serial process (E2).

And again:

I went to work to FNB of Belen, it was Jim … a family that owned it, Jim was the president, the chairman, and you know all of those, I can go and sit down in his office and say this deal doesn't make sense (E2).

Interestingly enough also bankers that never belong to First National bank talk about a Papen era:

> In the Papen days down in this small location, they would make the same choice, they would say okay as an independent bank we are only in Dona Ana county so where do we build our new branch and they'll build one and we are in a lot bigger geography so we say Dona Ana county doesn't really hit the ( ) so we are probably not going to put one in there and I am not saying that we won't I am just ( ) so I don't have a whole lot of input in those kind of things other than maybe show fact and figures and pointing in the right direction but the ultimate decision is with the higher level (E2).

And it's not only a matter of who actually makes the decision, but the social corporeal dimension also seems to be different:

> Southern NM has a very challenging geography, to have training, to have meetings, to have face to face stuff going on, so how do we do that, well we a lot of conference call going on, but what does that mean, you have a conference call, you don't have that face to face you don't see those verbal and non verbal clues…if you have a loan committee and people they can ask me question and go back and forth and that kind of things, on a serial approval process that we can't do (E2).

Moreover:

> The biggest thing that I think has to do with this is when you go to a serial process we lose the opportunity to train bankers, there is no committee environment, so how you young bankers start hearing questions that are commonly asked, start dissecting the deal, that's tough…in the environment that we are in the country today. It is hard to find business bankers and I think a lot of this is because they haven't been thought much in terms of experience (E2).

It is difficult not to think about Benjamin's "end of experience" in these words. In his work on storytellers, Benjamin, recollected in

Chapters 1 and 2, argues that the end of the experience coincides with the end of storytelling. Benjamin also talks about the practical function of stories, similarly to the war stories of Orr recollected in Chapter 2. Here the banker questions himself about the fact that by not sitting on the committee the young bankers do not gain the experience that prepares them to cope with the different situations of business banking.

## 5.5   Acquisitions

In this section we will hear fragments of storytelling about acquisitions. There is more than one acquisition involved in this story: there is the acquisition of First National Bank by First Security Corporation, the acquisition of First Security Corporation by Wells Fargo and the merger of Norwest and Wells Fargo, and indeed all the other acquisitions the interviewees came into contact during their careers.

The story of Wells Fargo in Las Cruces intertwines with the story of the merger between First National Bank of Dona Ana and First Security Corporation. Here is the account of a banker from the First National Bank side talking about how Wells Fargo came into town:

> A group came to town, they owned a bank called United New Mexico and they moved into Las Cruces I would say about 1990 their first building was, you know that building between the Red Lobster and Ride a Bike, that was their building... and Jim who is still with us ran United New Mexico and by 1995 or 1996 they sold out to a company called Norwest Bank which was a huge middle market bank, and shortly thereafter if you read the book it says Wells Fargo bought Norwest, actually Norwest took over Wells Fargo bank because Wells Fargo was struggling they had just a big merger in California with another huge bank I forget the name they were just sinking... customers of both banks left because they couldn't just get it together and so Norwest Bank actually took over but they kept the name because that logo the horses and buggy is in the top ten recognizable logo in the world... and that's why they kept the name I can still put out some of the forms on my computer when I am trying to do something and they will have the

Norwest sign up in the corner and the guy that runs the bank his name is Dick Kovacevich is a Norwest guy and rumors are that he is going to retire in 2008 and Stumpf... but that's how Wells Fargo came into Las Cruces (A1).

The merger between Wells Fargo and Norwest took place in November 1998: Norwest acquired Wells Fargo bank in a $31.7 billion deal, in what was referred to by O'Reilly, Pfeffer and Chang as a "merger of equals" (O'Reilly, Pfeffer and Chang, 2004). The name was then changed to Wells Fargo & Company in order to "capitalize on the 150 years history of Wells Fargo bank and on its trademark stagecoach" (Wikipedia, Wells Fargo, 2007) logo, one of the tenth most recognizable logos in the world and "a staple of the mythology of the American West" (*Stagecoach: Wells Fargo and the American West*, Free Press, 2007). Headquarters were moved to the San Francisco base of Wells Fargo, while Richard Kovacevich, former head of Norwest became president and CEO of the newly formed bank.

The merger is inscribed in a history of mergers that has produced an extensive body of literature in the management domain, among others I will cite is the work by Paul Hirsh (1986), as this deals with the theme of the mergers in the eighties from a cultural and communicational point of view.

The interviewees perceive the theme of mergers also as a historical feature of the nineties:

> (Boje): it is an amazing amount of organizations buying other organizations...
>
> (A1) It was very popular in the nineties to buy, but you don't see those mergers anymore.

What I would like to show here is that the experience of mergers for the people involved may vary according to several factors involving social and cultural aspects such as the recognition given by the new members, or their respect for the former team.

Talking about the Wells Fargo acquisition from the First National Bank side:

> When they [Wells Fargo] bought the bank, they actually bought First Security Corporation out of Utah, because they wanted to be

in Utah, and Colorado and somewhere else, we just happened to be there (A1).

But also:

We were really fortunate the way it came down because the people that were involved in this acquisition and competed against us had been some people from San Francisco, we may have not got that treatment but we were dealing with people from New Mexico that knew us, knew what we were about, gave us all the authority we needed to make the transition (C1).

And again:

So when we ( ) with Wells Fargo, very first thing I told about the acquisition team, was what I hear from you I am going to report to our folks and if it's different, if you are going to do something differently that what you are telling me I want to know it now because you won't have me to do it…and we kind of operated that way and they were very supportive and I didn't have any problem with them and they treated us very respectfully, because they understood that the success of this merger and it was a tough one because we had two banks, here in town competing with each other and it was a clash of cultures and there was the differences in the operating models, that needed to be brought together…I guess that they treated us the way they did…because they recognized what we had done (C1).

Unlike the First Security acquisition where:

There was a big concern about people losing their jobs and I remember asking one of the First Security people about that and they said no, nobody is going to lose their job, and that was not true (B1).

And in the word of another interviewee:

And we were just very close to leave, I know I was because I had made a lot of commitment to people and I said things and made

> promises, made representation to people on how things would be,
> and it didn't work out that way (C1).

These extracts are good examples of storytelling fragments that do not possess the beginning, middle and end, structure, but they are very significative of the way the tellers make sense of the situation. Such fragments do not show narrative properties identified by narratologists but are closer to Herrnstein Smith's definition of narrative recollected in Chapter 1. They are also very close to the "antenarrative" concept as defined by Boje. Storytelling extracts may sometimes allow the emergence of dimensions that would not emerge in consolidated narratives. The case of "and that was not true" and "and it didn't work out that way" are examples of what, in the last chapter, I will label as rough stories, rough materials. Such fragments show a very loose syntactic structure.

Recognition being a crucial issue, what is interesting to see, from a storytelling point of view, is that bankers from the acquisition team spontaneously expressed recognition for the former First National bankers:

> Those are the folks that made the bank (D2).

And also feel sympathetic with their frustration regarding the First Security acquisition in a sort of consolidated narrative of the event:

> When First Security bought them they went back in a lot of areas, computer, technology, ways of what we call analyzing accounts, just a lot of different things and that was part of the reason why they needed to finally get bought [First Security] (D2).

And:

> It was tough on those guys it really was (D2).

Here is the reconstruction of one of the bankers involved from First National Bank:

> We stepped back, on the process side of the bank which is pushing the wedges through and making them they were way behind us

we were ten years ahead of them on technology on the network-
ing and the customer they were ahead above us because they had
focused their attention on the network, the integration of the PCs,
into the service side of the business…but as pushing the paper
through and making the wedges coming through they were way
behind us (C1).

And again:

The transition we went through with First Security was an absolute
nightmare we had to step back with obsolete technology (C1).

This is true to the point that the Wells Fargo merger has been seen as
a survival and this has become a narrative from both sides, and also
among Wells Fargo members, as the following excerpts witness:

I have heard about First Security down here, Papen probably told
you a little bit about that hat sounded like it was a very rocky
process and this was kind like a savior when Wells Fargo came
in (E2).

From another Wells Fargo member:

I don't want to use it but it was kind of the knight coming in, hey
I am going to save everybody (D2).

And from another Wells Fargo member:

Who knows what would have happened to First Security I don't
know whether they would have been able to continue so it worked
out well, we jumped from where we were Norwest in Las Cruces
we really moved up in terms of our presence in Las Cruces (D2).

Storytelling is a powerful device in the understanding of how people
experience and frame events:

(A1) We owned the Tower building, we owned this building, we
owned north main and south main, we owned all these buildings
and when we sold the bank, a broker ((change the tone)) sold the

> bank from my cousin for First Security Corporation, Salt Lake
> City, Utah, and those cowboys came down and I was in charge
> of taking care of them, so I took them around and showed them
> all the branches and we went down to Anthony, kind of crappy
> looking and they asked how long is the lease and I said no lease
> we own it and they said how much do we own... THEY HAD
> NO CLUE.
>
> (Boje):  you said those cowboys, what does that mean?
>
> (A1)  I call them cowboys, I won't tell you what I really think of
> them, but I will never do business with that particular kind of
> persons again in my life I thought they were very unethical they
> cost us half of our life... we were fortunate we had Wells Fargo
> to step up...

We can see in this account the narrative of the rescue and saving, and
that of the rocky acquisition by the "cowboys": what is interesting is
that in this passage both consolidated narratives and rough material,
such as "they had no clue", coexist.

## 5.6   New lives

The actual conversion required preparation and time. Here is an
account from the Wells Fargo side:

> Our date I remember was in 2001 in the spring, because we were
> finishing up our new branch on El Paseo same time, we picked all
> the colors out I was involved in the plans and everything so it was
> fun, so we did that and that was the biggest thing I remember we
> converted on a Saturday and I was downtown at the motor bank
> just watching things to see how we converted, but it went very
> smoothly and part of that when we merged, when we bought First
> Security Wells did, that means the Santa Teresa location, Anthony,
> all the Las Cruces and Hatch, because that's where all the places
> were and then they also had Roswell so that all became part of
> Wells at that time, so it's a lot of work behind the scenes, a lot of
> getting ready, a lot of training of the folks that were with First Secu-
> rity to learn when you go looking at a checking account, here's
> how you go in an look at it, learning the new system and how to
> book the loans, how to open up accounts, all that stuff they need

to go through the training so just right there, every time you do a merger you are relearning the way of doing things (D2).

And:

It took more than one year to make the conversion, the actual flip over (D2).

And:

One big thing was the conversion of the system from First Security to the Wells Fargo and at some point you had to flip the switch and all the checking accounts, and all the savings, and all the loans they go from that system to the Wells Fargo system (D2).

And again:

You know we wanted to make sure that everything was done so the same day everybody... you make that flip over (D2).

The humans also have to flip:

You are trying to flip them (D2).

And:

They have an attitude, you know I am going to work for this folks I need to make that flip, make the flip to be part of Wells Fargo (D2).

"Flip" is the term used to mean both the conversion of the systems, and the experience of the people involved: the language of the systems becomes the language of the people.

Here is another banker from Wells Fargo talking about the Norwest–Wells Fargo merger. Notice that when talking about mergers and acquisition people often use metaphors like marriage and divorce. Emphasis here is on different corporate cultures:

But it took longer to quit thinking I was Norwest and start thinking I was Wells Fargo because it's a weird marriage, because what happened was that the head of our company at Norwest was in Minnesota and our main office was based in Minneapolis and the main office at the Wells Fargo is based in San Francisco well, the head of our company moved to San Francisco so that's sound like Norwest took over, but actually Wells was a little big bigger of an entity at that time in terms of market capitalization so that's sounds like Wells Fargo bought Norwest so it's kind of weird how it shook out... but we on the Norwest side it just felt like a lot more, I guess my sense of the culture was that Norwest was a lot more concerned about people and more not only team members but also the communities that we were in (E2).

And again:

I think there were 5 big mergers announced in 1998 and Wells Fargo acquired, Wells Fargo and Norwest merger and they don't say that one acquired the other, they always refers to it as mergers of equals because they were pretty comparable in size and the philosophy were very different and what's kind of... to this point I mean it takes a long time to work through processes and make the same systems and creating a common culture and all those things and we are still not through it but you but the things that I think Wells Fargo brought to the table were technology, they did a lot of metropolitan type banking, they weren't really concerned about smaller communities I don't think so, they tried to do things very efficiently, very budget based and so they would operate on what we call silos you have all these different or departments that specialize in I am going to do commercial real estate loans and that's all we are going to focus on and then this next side they only work on cash management products for business customers, that kind of things... whereas the Norwest philosophy was very much community based... we were very geographically dispersed and the local bank presence were giving the autonomy to deliver products and services based on what they thought it was best and there has been a combination of that, but the way we do it right now, we have got a lot of partners, our local people are expected to get to know the community, get to know the players and introduce things to them to the extent that they can but then they bring in partners to do the expertise on the subject matter (E2).

Of course the community involvement is not the same as in the old era. Here is an account from the First National Bank side:

> They know, Wells Fargo knows that they have to have a commitment to the community; they have to contribute to such things as the chamber of commerce and the university and things of that nature, but NO, NO concept of Mr Papen, NO (A1).

And again from another interviewee:

> Wells Fargo comes out from the standpoint of supporting the communities but it's not … and there is a mindful commitment there, but it's not 24/7 and for obvious reasons I mean we have shareholders that are publicly traded company and the end of the day the analysts don't want to hear about how much we gave to charity and how many chamber of commerce meetings we went to, or how many open houses we went to, they want to know return on assets, they want to know, price earnings and what our next twelve months are going to look like, and all those kind of thing (C1).

It is a major shift from community bank to Wells Fargo:

> We don't make any big loan decision here, we don't make any investment decision here, we do make some personnel decision based on company policies, you know, but they are not life changing decisions, if they got a three million loan and they want to make it and everybody here is behind it and then they sent it to the next level and if they don't like it it's not going to happen but that's all right too, you have to have everything in place, it's a different philosophy (A1).

It is interesting to notice here the "but it's all right too": the third time of narration that we have previously encountered throughout the chapter.

It is a different life within a different existential condition. In the next excerpt we find again the two poles of narration and the third time: "which is fine, it's all right" and the final "you kind of miss", which express the emergent and rough material of experience.

> Looking back at that right now and the way they do things, it was
> completely... I am sure small banks are still run that way today to
> a certain degree, but... I don't know. I have never been in their
> decision-making process, in today's world, I have no decision-
> making and that is what is hard for me to EXIST with because
> I was so used of making them and so was Tom and Ben. I don't
> have any authority to do anything, I can't... which is fine... it's
> all right, it's just different, it's just a different life. YOU KIND OF
> MISS NOT MAKING DECISIONS (A1).

There are moments in which socialized and constructed narratives
relax and experience emerges in its intimate and sometimes nostal-
gic form. Storytelling performs in these cases a soothing function as
expressed by Gabriel and articulated in Chapter 2.

We can't really compare community banks with a bank like Wells
Fargo, one of the interviewees says:

> Well, when we start talking about Wells Fargo we have to remem-
> ber that we are talking about the fifth largest bank in US they
> have products and services I don't even know what they are, for
> example the biggest customer that I had during my days and he's
> currently the biggest customer of Wells Fargo bank, they don't
> even let him bank in Las Cruces anymore, he lives here, he has
> his business here but his loans are handled out of California,
> or Phoenix and all his investment products are handled in Salt
> Lake City, so I wouldn't even see him here other than we are
> good friends and he tells me what is going on and what they are
> doing (A1).

Another interviewee from the First National Bank side offers this
reconstruction:

> We were basically a family owned business from the beginning
> and you know the history of all that, family owned businesses
> usually disintegrate, this one didn't but it wasn't an easy process
> to get through and First Security was just a bigger version of us
> now Wells Fargo, Norwest I think was in a similar situation before
> Dick Kovacevich got involved in the late 80 and kind of turned
> the company around, cleaned house and made some changes in

management which is not an easy process to get through and so that company moved, it made the change and had a paradigm shift (C1).

And again:

Old Norwest started as a small regional bank and they had that same kind of orientation that we had when we were a small community bank that didn't have ... we had 300 shareholders but 200 out of them were employees or former employees and that wasn't a publicly traded company, you had to fight to get any stock, and Norwest kind of evolved in the same way, they went through the Ag crisis of the eighties (C1).

Which leads to:

We had a paradigm shift with technology and risk management issues that required us to take to the next level some of the people we brought in to get it to this critical mass at this level couldn't get to the next level it's like playing sports and I suspect that, and I know from outside looking in First Security had the same problem because they really didn't change anything in the management, we sold as a way to make the changes and let somebody else do them (C1).

And:

They [Wells Fargo] could do things that a bank of our size at that point of time, we couldn't do, we didn't have the infrastructure, we didn't have the expertise, the financial resources to put the infrastructures in place, it's the chicken and the egg kind of thing we would have had to rethink our strategy completely and go into an acquisition there were two ways to do it, go public, starting acquiring other banks which would have put the family at risk with their stock to market conditions which they didn't have or sell, those were the two options, so this small community banks they have a niche right now but the one failure I think of bankers in general has been that we think we are and our ego gets in

> play and we begin doing things that are outside our box and we should ... the small community banks if they have a niche and they stay in that and don't get outside that niche and customers it's too big for what they can do best is fine but they won't do that (C1).

It is a consolidated narrative synthesized in the last sentence:

> You make a lot of commitments in a organization setting to get the band started to play the music, but they may not be able to play the music for the next deal (C1).

The point I will try to make here is that storytelling portrays both the making sense of an event such as an acquisition through a consolidated narrative and the challenge and emergence of experience, emotions and memories through story fragments that I will label rough stories in the seventh chapter.

Here are some examples of emergence:

> For example our pin used to have that circle on it and they put a diamond every five years and Ben and I had too many diamonds ... I still have my pin ... well you just have to go on, to move on, it's different, like being divorced, starting over again, like a new life when we first did the First Security deal they told us that everything was going to be wonderful, actually it didn't work out (A1).

And from the same interviewee:

> I will never forget the day we were all at the double eagle restaurant and ((goes and picks up a clock on the shelf)) ... gave me this clock February second 1998, ... It was a marvelous time in my life and I thought I was rich, but I wasn't but that's all right (A1).

There are three movements in the last extract, the first is the "it was a marvelous time" narrative which finds its development in the "I thought I was rich", the second is the challenging of the narrative into "but I wasn't" and the third is the actual inscription of the one over the other, which results into "but it's all right".

And from another interviewee:

> I enjoyed it, it was a tremendous challenge it thought me a lot about the human condition over the years and I have used that phrase a number of time but it really is true, one thing about the business that it's still absolutely fascinating is that it's a huge laboratory in human behavior and you can see just about any way there is to either make a success or screw something up in all aspects of life, because we see it all, we see the good decisions and what it leads to and we see the bad decisions and what they led to, I had to live with (C1).

And again:

> Not many people understand, I know you guys understand what I am talking about here and most of the people don't, they don't know and I consider myself extremely fortunate to have been able to live through all this because basically I came from a point in my career when I first started in this organization where everything was done on a ledger and you had girls, girls because men wouldn't do it, it was a woman job to do it to go through the deposit slip and posting to ledger cards and then at the end of the month cut the ledgers in two and keep the half to do the balance for the next month and mail the other half out that's the kind of technology that was in place when I first started in this organization, we used to file all the checks and the fact that I and I attribute a lot just to the opportunity I had to go to school because when I graduate from NMS I was John and I were, because Tom wasn't here yet, many people in the bank didn't had any college education and I had an accounting background and a degree in finance and I was able to take that stuff from the classroom and make it work at the bank so this basically was a laboratory for me and the very first guy that I hired when they put me in charge of the operations was my old accounting professor I brought him in as an auditor because we didn't have an audit function, they didn't have...everything was done on a cash basis, accounting done, they didn't know from one day to the next, where they made the

money at the end of the month they kind of forced the balances and I was able to migrate through all that … there wouldn't be another opportunity like that (C1).

It is the uniqueness of a work life, of a work life experience.

Here is a short conversation between Professor Boje and one of the interviewees from First National Bank.

> (Boje): you had this status in New Mexico, big time
> (C1)  WE DID …
> (Boje):  But I don't know if these people here have the same status you know …
> (C1)  Well, that's what I was alluding to before, and I have thought about all that a lot …

This short extract brings us to the level of personal and intimate experience that is difficult to express and delineate, when we talk about First National bank, we can talk about the decision-making processes and technology but there is an excess of sense for the people that were working for that bank that cannot be captured in any description. There are different levels of analysis: we can see processes from outside or we can try to capture what those processes mean for the people involved. In the last extracts I have tried to delineate this intimate landscape.

What is interesting is that both the interviewees from First National Bank and the ones from Wells Fargo have, during their careers, being faced with such an experience, being on one side or the other.

Here are some accounts from the Wells Fargo side:

> It really takes time, send folks out for the training, depending on what you did, so you learn our systems, you learn the way we do things … to get everything ready before we actually … the signs went up, we had them covered and we take the covers down and ((makes a gesture with the hands)) (D2).

A rational explanation of acquisitions:

> Growth. You know bottom line building that return for the shareholders, each acquisition we are hoping is going to bring more

revenue more bottom line in stockholder, that's what we are around for, stockholder wealth (D2).

And talking about Norwest–Wells Fargo merger:

Norwest had a good identity but it was little bit more difficult down here because they were mainly up in the Midwest, Minnesota, Wisconsin, the Dakotas that type of stuff, so that may have been a little bit more difficult down in this area for people to grasp what's Norwest about, but Wells Fargo, I mean watch a movie and here it's the stagecoach (D2).

This is a peculiar aspect of the Wells Fargo acquisition in New Mexico, as the Wells Fargo logo and mythology fits into the history of this place, generating a sort of reconstructed and retrofitted continuity. I will talk about this aspect in Chapter 7.

Here is an account from one of the bankers from First National Bank.

When we first converted to Wells Fargo they had us to watch a 20 minutes videotape with all the history and all the things that they did and where they have been you know it's all promotion stuff but they have a nice museum at the bottom floor of their building and I happened to be there on an Amigo trip and ((LAUGHS)) and I went across the street and went into the museum and it's pretty interesting shows you all kind of things, it goes back to the early days of California when they had horses and the buggies and the gold, talking about shipping the money from New York to San Francisco and all the goods to the gold mines (A1).

## 5.7  New bankers

In this section are a collection of experiences of the bankers from Wells Fargo in Las Cruces; most of them are direct experiences, with a few extracts from former First National bankers talking about the new context.

Here is the account from one of the bankers from Wells Fargo:

> My history goes back to the State National Bank in El Paso, Texas, that's where I started, and that's the bank that have started back in the 1870s and it was one of the old independent banks, so that was kind of neat because that was back in the days where we still had unit banking so each bank was its own separate bank, there was no branch banks like we have now ... and then when I left it became part of what was known as M-Bank and that was just the start back then of the bank consolidation started to come, 1988 and then I went to a bank in El Paso called Sun West bank which through all the gyrations is now Bank of America (D2).

The theme of the mergers is a constant feature of the new bankers' experience:

> That was when the big mergers started taking place, and Sun West the bank that became SunWest was a local bank called American Bank of Commerce and it got purchased by SunWest and then got bough by Boatman, kind of strange we had a boat for a logo and we are in a desert, so they didn't use it, they still used the Sun West name but they were part of Boatman, and it became another bank and then it eventually became Bank of America, now I can't remember the bank that was in between Boatman, but it went though a lot of gyrations (D2).

As shown also in the next extract:

> You know when I came here when it was Norwest, United New Mexico had just been purchased about one year earlier by Norwest so when I came here the folks here were still trying to adjust to the Norwest changes and then about three years later we got bought or really we bought Wells Fargo, Norwest bought Wells Fargo and we kept the name, but going back to the Sun West days I was there and then left for the First National Bank of Albuquerque which then got bought by First Security and then I came down here with Norwest then Norwest actually bought Wells Fargo but we kept the name because they had a better brand recognition (D2).

It is a very fragmented work history from State National in El Paso through Sun West, First National Bank of Albuquerque, First Security, Norwest into Wells Fargo

Likewise another member of Wells Fargo bank says:

> I will tell you about my background, you know one of the things that we really talk about with our teams, because we do merger and acquisitions all the time, some of the people tend to, you know there is a transition period there, but when you come in and start talking to the people they have a tendency to think that you have always been with Wells Fargo and I kind of talk to them a little bit, we were all assimilated at one point, I mean none of us started out, I mean there are probably a few that did but I was born and raised in Hobbs which in the south east corner of the state I don't know whether you are familiar with the state geography but it's pretty much east from here, about three and a half hour, right on the Texas border, and grew up there and took my first job in banking at seventeen when I was still in high school and I worked in the mailroom of a bank called First National Bank of Lee County and you know (E2).

The histories of companies' changes are intertwined with personal life recollections:

> And after I graduated from New Mexico State with a degree in Finance I got out in 1985 and I actually wanted to stay in the area and talk with different banks and talked to Ben's bank at that time, and they really didn't have anything and you know how it is in those days there was a lot of demand from the student side to get a job as opposed to the employers, it was kind of tough to get a job, my mum had, she worked in the legal profession and she worked in the bank in Hobbs that I worked at and she got out and started selling real estates and did very well so she encouraged me to try that so I sold real estate here for three years right after college (E2).

And:

> My wife's grandmother in Albuquerque, we found out that she had cancer…and spent the last year of her grandmother's life near her

I ended up going up there and started working for a bank called
First National Bank of Belen... And my first loan request I remember it was a little guy came in and he smelled like alcohol first thing
in the morning and he said: I need to borrow 45 dollars (E2).

And:

So I went to work for UNM and within 12 months Norwest came
in and bought UNM and FNB of Belen so either way I was going to
be part of the Norwest Wells Fargo family and so that's how I got
into it and I started working for UNM in 1994 and I went to work
up there, we call it a store manager today I was a retail branch
manager (E2).

And again:

And then I was in a meeting up there and the president of the bank
in Hobbs which was in the same building that I worked, it was a
Norwest bank at that time, but it was in the same building that I
worked in when I was in High School... so we ended up moving to
Hobbs and I worked as a business banker for three years from 1994
to 1997 and in 1997... but that only lasted a year because of the
president of the bank in Alamogordo quit and they offered me that
job so I came down to Alamogordo in the beginning on 1999 and
about that time it was when we were transitioning from Norwest
into Wells Fargo so I... worked down in Alamogordo from 1999
until 2003 and in 2003 our bank in Farmington and the way that
has kind of worked in our company and the way it has worked for
me is that I did not really step up and said give me more, but I
think if you are doing a good job and this is the way I look at it,
and that's the way I look at people under me... if you are doing a
good job you can probably do a good job over a bigger area and
have a greater influence on what I am trying to do, so I did a
little bit of ( ) Ruidoso and then got bigger and got to Alamogordo
and got even bigger and went to Farmington and now I am in
charge of all southern New Mexico so the Farmington move was
in 2003 and I went up there to basically run that bank and the
bank was acquired in 2000 so there again we had some of the
issues of people saying I don't know if I want to do this and that

kind of thing but they wanted to get the paychecks but they were not willing to make the changes to the way we did things so we had a lot of that to go through (E2).

We can see that in both experiences there is a beginning at a First National or community bank with a high number of changes. Mergers and acquisitions characterize experiences of new bankers, and organizations are made up of people coming from the most different experiences. Here is the account of the United New Mexico acquisition by Norwest seen from somebody who did not belong to UNM but worked for Norwest:

[United New Mexico–Norwest] and they referred as being dipped in blue because Norwest had blue colors on their loan policy books and you have to think UNM loan policy was probably like this ((demonstrates with his fingers)) Norwest was like that ((demonstrates with his fingers)) so it was the dipping in blue, now with Wells Fargo we don't know because it changes, we just leave it online, we don't attempt to print (D2).

And the same interviewee about the First National bank–First Security acquisition:

Now on the side here, First National Bank of Dona Ana County, that bank started in the early nineteen then I forgot in what year it got bought by First Security...it was a total change for them, and that's when you talk about what's like about to go through, because this folks, you know they had been the independent bank forever forever forever then all of the sudden, bum, here comes new loan policy, structured way of doing things, you know, reporting out (D2).

And again:

You have to remember back in those days First National Bank they were the dominant bank in this market, they always been, they were the largest bank, everything...so here we are and we are coming in and showing them, hey here's the Wells Fargo way, so number one is totally different from what they are used to, you got policies, procedures, structural changes, just you name it, it was a total change for them, even though they were part of the First Security organization, they have not been in the big corporate world really for a long time and then to go to a Wells Fargo, where we are even more of the large corporate structure than even a First Security (D2).

And here general considerations about mergers and acquisitions:

You know for the person that has the right frame of mind, it's a honeymoon deal, you know I am going to be, that's what I look at, think of it when you go to a new business and you start, it's a honeymoon for a while you are learning, life's great, I don't really have lot of the burden, but guess what, after a while like every honeymoon it stops and then reality sets in, you know what, you have been here for four months now, and like a merger, we have gone through the merger you have done the training, okay, when are we going to start with, we are in the business like everybody is in the business, we want to do what is good for our customers but we also want to do what's good for our stockholders (D2).

Wells Fargo corporate culture has a strong customer orientation:

We still feel for being in business banking you have to be able to talk to the customers, that's our philosophy (D2).

And another view from another interviewee:

But the way I look at it, it's that you always have to balance your commitment to the shareholder and your commitment to your customers and your commitment to our team member those are the three constituencies that we have got to and you can't say I am going to do everything for the team member because then your customers I mean if we did everything for our team members we would not be open on Saturdays we would be closed at three o'clock, I mean, and that's not good for the shareholders, and it's not good for our customers so you have to have a balance on all that it makes sense, we pride ourselves of being a retail bank and what retail store is not open on Saturdays (E2).

And in the words of one of the former First National bankers:

> Most of them are pretty new, they haven't been with the bank a long time, turnover is kind of high in Wells Fargo world because they have such great expectations for their people, Wells Fargo is more of a sales company so if you come in and go to work at Wells Fargo bank they tell you that you are going to be responsible to have so many sales per week or per month and per year, that's why sometimes you see a big line out here and you see a guy at the counter and they are talking, well that teller, and I hate to say that because this is not the way I would run a bank, but the teller job is to sell, he is selling a debit card, a credit card, a line of credit, something, or get a referral, you don't have to do the selling, but that's their job to make referrals, get a loan to your kid to go to college, get you a debit card, credit card, line of credit, overdraft protection and on and on and on, they got you a whole list of stuff that they are going to sell you, their philosophy is that if they can get you to have six products, you can never afford to leave it costs you too much money to leave and it's too much so you are going to stay here pay the fees and do what you have to do, which is a different philosophy I mean it not the same (A1).

And again from the Wells Fargo side:

> You go to the community banks, they used to be commercial lenders, guess what they are now, they are business bankers, we don't call our locations branches, they are stores, we have just began here in Las Cruces we are open Saturday full banking services inside from nine to one and the reason is what do we do, we provide retail services for the most part, so why shouldn't we be open when a lot of folks have the time to come in … we are very much retail oriented … a sales organization that provides financial services (D2).

It turns out that part of this selling orientation comes from Dick Kovacevich (Wells Fargo CEO) mentality:

> It started in the Norwest days but it has been accelerated when Wells Fargo and Norwest came together … that's Dick Kovacevich

he was the one that put this mentality of we have stores, we want folks to come in and…what we are going to do, we will talk to them about what we can do for them to make them better off financially and everybody has goals towards making our customers have our products we are a sales organization, so we are going to talk to you when you come in about our products and services with the goal of they are going to make you better off financially (D2).

Wells Fargo discourse is that of a bank that is able to bring different services and products to local level. Here are the accounts of Wells Fargo bankers:

We are a big bank but we are pretty much local, we tend to we can out-national the locals and out-local the nationals (D2).

And:

If we find a big one [customer] we have the avenue to take them to another part of Wells and they can get helped (D2).

And again:

First Security would have more products and services than a First National, we bring a lot more to the table, but we do it in a way where we are still a lot involved in the community, we want our bankers to be out visiting their customers, we want them outside the bank, we want them at the customer's business, talking about hey I want let you know how you can be better off financially by using this particular product and that's our goal, we want customer to be better off financially, investment, we are going to find a broker, right next door from here, we can bring him in he can do anything a Merrill Lynch…we have got an investment manager trust over here, we have a money manager on site, so if you want, out of certain dollar level for us to manage your investments we will go through it, we will put the criteria together you give us your investment tolerances we will manage your money for you (D2).

From a communicational point of view it is interesting to notice that part of the discourse of large banks is "we are like a local bank", big banks want to look local not global, as global seems to be perceived far from the local need. HSBC for example prides itself on being the world's local bank.

For a communicational point of view perspective on these aspects see Koller (2007). Koller argues that glocalization is part of a branding strategy for banking institutions. In the new corporate world the importance of communication is widely recognized, communication is used as a strategic tool in marketing campaigns. Boje has often time insisted on the dangers of the appropriation of storytelling tools by corporate companies. Storytelling has become in today's corporate world a strategic tool in the branding processes (many marketing campaign are based on stories), in the organization of work (to motivate employees managers tell effective stories) and so on. This approach sometimes even uses the work done by scholars in the organizational narrative domain, but by reducing this approach in an objectivistic and mechanistic way to achieve effective communication.

It is interesting here to recollect the words of one of the First National bankers when they asked him about an acquisition of a small bank. From this short storytelling excerpt we find out how small local communities may perceive big banks:

> Once they asked me to go to Clovis, why do you guys want to buy a bank in a little town? We have too much of those 800 numbers for people in a small town, they want service, they don't want to call all over the world (A1).

Returning to differences in terms of structures between community banks and large banks:

> It's just a different way, this [First National Bank of Dona Ana] was an independent bank that didn't have to report to anybody but their own board and that board was all local community folks, First Security it get more decentralized, now you have to go to Salt Lake City for lot of your decisions, because that's where they are based out of, Wells Fargo, we are that much bigger, we bring more structure, but we still have a huge philosophy of relationship banking, if we didn't I wouldn't be here, the bankers wouldn't be here,

we would say if you got a small business loan, here's where you need to send it, but we are here, because that's our belief, we want to bring the power of our bigness and all our technology and all the things that we can do and bring it to other communities that we are in, a First National Bank of Dona Aria County could do couple of things mainly to folks, they can make loans, they can have saving accounts CDs [certificate of deposit] and checking, and they had some trust services, not much and that was pretty much a lot of the independent banks what they could do and if you look some of the independent banks that are still in town here that's pretty much what they do, if they have got investments they are using a third party, if they have analyses, sweep accounts…they are using a third-party, they are not doing it in house, because is not cost effective for them but we are very, very much, we just bring all the bigness and the greatness that Wells Fargo can do for customers, but we bring it in a relationship local level (D2).

And here is how centralization is viewed in one interview from the First National bank's side:

They [Wells Fargo] make the decisions on top and it's filtered down I can go up to Telshor right now and somebody in Albuquerque made this decision and they don't know, they just make decisions that go across the border for everybody and that's all right too (A1).

There are a lot of differences as we have seen in terms of structures, in terms of orientations, in terms of involvement, in terms of products offered, and in terms of leaders:

Dick Kovacevich, who the chairman of the board is always saying you know you rent the position (E2).

And their personality:

But Frank, his personality, you could not separate the bank from his personality and John is pretty much that way and I was the guy to make people mad trying to make that work, I have a lot of emotions about it but I think it's better, how should I put it I think that I always known that there was a better way to do all this, but Frank you could not separate his personality from the bank and he was just one case in point, if you went into Texas and you interviewed some of the family members of some of those old community banks it's the same thing, in New Mexico, same thing, you couldn't separate the personality from the leadership from the bank and you could tell if you were invited to a cocktail party, and this is absolute truth, if you were invited to a cocktail party and you didn't know anything about it and you went to the party you would know who they were banking with for who was at that party and it has evolved from that and at Wells Fargo is a publicly traded company that's basically at the mercy of the analysts so Dick Kovacevich is not, although he has tremendous influence psychologically on what happens his name is not synonymous with Wells Fargo (C1).

What is important for me is to show how personal reconstructions expressed in the storytelling always portrays a double orientation, toward a socialized we:

> You know it has been 26 years and I enjoyed and if I go another ten years I think that will be about it, it is a lot of stuff there is a lot of process to what we do and you know we were federally regulated, so that puts a lot of pressure, whatever you want to say and that we have got to do things the right way, we have to stick to our loan policies and a lot of our loan policies are dictated by what the regulators want us to do as a banking organization…but it has been fun, I really enjoyed, it has been no days are the same you are always talking to a new customer, you learn something new about the business (D2).

And the emergence of story fragment that witness alternative paths:

> Sure who wouldn't like that and those was fun days, that was more of a…you kind of shoot from the hip kind of deal, there are a lot of stories that goes back into those days (D2).

This last sentence is a very significative one, as it posits in a simple form the creation of a world through storytelling. What is even more significative is that it is said by one of the members of the new bank.

# 6
## From Empirical Research to Discussion

In the second part of the work I have presented the empirical research I have performed in Las Cruces, New Mexico. In Chapter 4 I have provided an account of how the research has unfolded, and how I actually got involved with the research: with the community bank and the bankers.

The research basically arose from almost randomly related episodes: I decided to do an exploratory study at the bank I opened my account at, which was 20 meters from my house. I interviewed one of the bankers and the next day in the canteen Professor Boje saw Professor Loveland and told him I wanted to do research on banking in Las Cruces. Loveland told me I should definitely contact John Papen, who had been one of his students, who could give me information on the history of banking in Las Cruces and about his uncle Frank. It turned out that the bank Frank Papen contributed to shaping in the sixties had been sold after his death to a Salt Lake City bank and later bought by the bank I had started to investigate. Another randomly connected event was finding the Leon Metz book *Southern New Mexico Empire*, which is the story of Frank Papen's bank, in the bookstore. I had bought and read that book before knowing that Frank Papen and the banker I had interviewed were related.

It was, however, through the interview with John Papen that the research and my research experience took a solid turn. In Chapter 4 I talk about the dense storytelling he offered us. Professor Boje and I were fascinated by such a refined articulation and recollection of dates, people, significative events paired by the showing of articles, objects and the premises of the bank with the murals and pictures of its past presidents.

This interview constituted one of the most important materials of the research. The research is based on the material collected with five main interviewees, divided into two groups: one is that of the bankers that were managing the bank before the acquisitions and the other group is that of the new managing team. Several formal and informal interviews were made with these bankers. The transcribed materials in Chapter 5 are the result of the transcription and editing of those interviews: but only a small portion of the interviews has been used.

The analyzed material also included the book by Leon Metz, the bank's newsletter and the archival material of the Rio Grande Historical Collection, together with the brochures of the new bank and website information about it. Extracts from these materials are also shown in Chapter 5.

In the fifth chapter I have exposed the material following a distinction in thematic areas, from the beginning of the bank to its actual situation, through the lens of the storytelling performed by the bankers and the storytelling material analyzed. The methodology used reflects both the impressive work done by Professor Boje in the field and personal adaptations. I was influenced in particular by Boje's two works of 1991 and 1994 about storytelling organizations recollected in Chapter 2 (in the first, he collected stories from an office supply firm as they spontaneously arose while in the second he collected stories from the archive of the Disney corporation) and his claim for the need of antenarrative research in his 2001 book. (Antenarrative has been paired also with the theoretical sensitivity of Professor Jedlowski, toward the subject, memory and experience.)

Chapter 5 is thus a collection of stories both from archives and from first-hand interviews edited around specific themes. The story is the story of a bank; a community bank that has been managed in a certain way for several years and that has been bought, first by one bank and then by a second. It is an interesting story, which is part of the wider economic and social history of the United States.

However, it is not the content of this history that matters to me, as this is only the landscape in which the storytelling sits. To me, what is interesting is the storytelling itself, more than its content. What happened is in fact told, it is told by the protagonists of the story, by an historian, it is told in newsletters, in brochures and so on. The story of the bank becomes to me the story of all the stories that its actors have been telling to themselves, to their colleagues, to their friends and families, and the story of the stories that are intertwined with these stories.

Everybody does not tell the stories in the same way, however. Stories are inextricably tied to personal experience, characters and events that appear in one story may not appear in others. Moreover, stories create worlds of possibilities, of intimate connections and emotional impacts.

In the Chapter 5 we found two different types of voice: that of the old managers and that of the new managers. The stories told share some aspects in common but they diverge on other aspects. What emerged in the fragments is, in the first place, the difference between conversational and spontaneous storytelling and written and thoughtful storytelling. Conversational and spontaneous excerpts tend to be more fragmented, lacking the beginning, middle and end structure described by narratologists. Written and polished storytelling tends to eliminate incongruences and retrospectively arrange events in a thoughtful manner. Also, in conversational storytelling, some aspects may be omitted or glossed in order to smooth out ambiguities. Glossing is a term I took from Boje's 1991 article mentioned in Chapter 2.

Some of the theory of Chapters 1 and 2 appears in the comments found in the excerpts, for example the idea of loose definition of story and narrative treated in Chapter 1, or the glossing and terse storytelling mechanisms of Chapter 2. We have seen, in the fifth chapter, storytelling at play as a sense-making device when interviewees frame the differences between the old way of managing the bank and the new way. Some of them plot this evolution as being historically based while others plot it in a large versus small bank conflict. The same can be said about the different frame provided by the loyalty of Frank Papen to the employees compared to the performance objectives exposed by some of the managers.

Another aspect which stems from the theory discussed in part one is the different function of storytelling in organizations. When talking about loan committee structures compared to centralized structures interviewees agree on the fact that people are not trained in terms of experience. Storytelling holds in this case both a practical, instructional function and an identitarian function. Communitarian function is also provided by the coffee tradition, in which the managing team would gather before making any important decision.

One novel aspect that has emerged is that the recognition of the stories, "they knew what we were about", from the acquiring team leads to a different ending in the acquisition process. Wells Fargo members recognize not only the stories of the old bank, the epic of the golden age, but also the tragedy of the difficult experience with First Security. They seem to accept the frustration and the pain that accompanied such a process as demonstrated by the sentence "it was hard on those folks". A new narrative is then produced: that of the knights coming in and saving the bank. But for the old members life will never be the same and the flips (mechanistic term used by the acquiring team) are for them new marriages and new lives. They tend to produce rational explanations, but, oftentimes, personal life experience emerges, with strong impact.

In the next chapter I will concentrate my attention on this aspect, and on the personal reinscription of we-narratives over I-fragments. Storytelling will then become a way of coping with a new reality with a soothing function as described by Gabriel. The new aspect that emerged from Chapter 5 is precisely in the duality of collective stories, where we-experience is at play together with I-fragments, where storytelling tends to give voice to intimate and often conflicting feelings.

There is also the aspect of the collective memory, which emerged clearly in the fifth chapter. Collective memory is at work for example in the refrains of "Frank was not a banker", the "Anthony miracle" and "The tower". These are stories of the old bank that are shared and recognized by all the members of the bank and to a larger extent also outside the bank: Papen's figure, the community bank era and that particular way of banking. But all these elements interact in each account at different levels and to different degrees. What is interesting to notice is that the interviews clearly confirm what the seminal work of Halbwachs and Namer posits, that is to say that that collective memory is a social construction and this social construction is articulated retrospectively through discourse interaction (Jedlowski, 2007; Middleton and Edwards, 1990).

The examples abovementioned solve exactly this function. But there are also other kinds of artifacts that activate such collective memory, for example the pictures of the presidents recollected in one of the interviews, or Papen's memorial in front of the bank.

Another novel aspect connected with storytelling is the difference between the first and second group in the way the interviewees talked about themselves and their organizations. The language seemed to change between the two groups: the language of the second group is closer to the language of the bank, the organization and its standardization. If the second group of bankers describe changes following mergers as "flips", the first group describes them in terms of "marriages" and "new lives".

Finally we started to apprehend that these people live among a number of stories: the stories of the past as collectively recollected; the stories that are written and codified; the emergence of personal and fragmented stories; the stories that the new bank strategically produces, and so on. This aspect will be the object of the following chapter.

# Part III
# Coming Back to Theory

# 7
# Living Among Stories: Consolidated Narratives and Rough Fragments

In this chapter I will make several considerations on the case treated and I will outline a research path for future projects. I will focus in particular on the aspects that emerged from the research itself and constitute the novelty of my work. Several considerations have been made already on the excerpts in Chapters 5 and 6, the aim of this chapter is not to reproduce those considerations but rather to focus on the aspects that cannot find the support of the theory of the first part of the book and thus need further development in order to be inscribed in a discourse on organizations. The context, as already pointed out, is that of communication and storytelling perspective in the organizational field. The idea is that of studying organizational phenomena and organizations themselves "from within" (Shotter, 2006). In April 2006, I presented my project at a conference on "Polyphony and dialogism as a way of organizing" held at the University of Essex, UK. One of the convenors, Professor John Shotter, gave an inspiring speech on Bakhtin's ideas, whose abstract I quote hereafter:

Traditionally language has been thought of as an already established, self-contained system of linguistic communication that sets out a set of rules or social conventions that people make use of in expressing themselves. In this account, what I will call the Cartesian account of language, people understand the linguistic representations contained or encoded in each other's sentences. However, another account – articulated by Bakhtin (1981, 1984, 1986) among a number of others, such as Wittgenstein, Vygotsky, and Merleau-Ponty – is of a much more dynamic, participatory, relational kind. In it, language and the world are intertwined in a chiasmic relation with each other, in which we are shaped just as much, if not more, by the world, as the world by us. Thus, to switch to this very different view of language is also to switch to a very different view of the world in which we live: it is to see it as a living, dynamic, indivisible world of events that is also still coming into being. In this view, we understand another person's utterances in terms of the bodily responses, the felt tendencies, they spontaneously arouse in us, responses that relate or orient us both toward them and toward events occurring in our shared surroundings. In other words, language is not a system for use by individuals to give shared expression to already clearly conceived significations, but is a way of organizing shared or sharable signi-fications between us for always another first time – each utterance is a once-occurrent event of being.

(Bakhtin, 1993)

In a published article, Shotter (2006) distinguishes between thinking "from within" and "from the outside", or between "withness" and "aboutness" thinking. Language represents an interesting paradigm in this move. As Shotter points out,

in the recent past (and still among many cognitive scientists), the main function of language is thought to be that of conveying our thoughts to another person in the form of a 'mental representa-tion', a *picture* as it were. And to *understand* the other person's utterance, we must 'get the picture'! Hence we study sentence *forms* to try to *represent* their *content*. Bakhtin's (1986) approach could not be more different. Rather than seeking meaning in terms of *patterns of already spoken words*, i.e. in what is said, he seeks it in our very *words in their speaking*, i.e. in our embodied uttering of them, as we utter them...In other words what Bakhtin brings to our attention here in describing the nature of our active, respon-sive understandings, is what almost everyone who has written on the activities of living beings that grow in irreversible time has brought to our attention: that is it not their spatial arrangements at different instants in time, but the *sequential ordering*, or the *time-ordering*, of events as they unfold, that is of crucial importance in all such processes – along with the fact that all such living and growing sequences are always *incomplete*, and thus as such, in their unfolding moments, they always inevitably 'point forward' future possibilities in some way.

(Shotter, 2006, pp. 590–591)

## 7.1   Between social determinacy and the uniqueness of experience

This is the very essence of Bakhtin's idea; being in continuous relation with the world, Bakhtin affirms that every utterance is dialogic. Every utterance is directed toward both the object, the content and the relationship, and this is perpetuated in every response. Every individual is immersed in this constant dialog at different levels. What is important for this work are both the continuous reference to the other and the idea that utterances represent events in themselves.

The first consideration we have to make is that the other in not simply our interlocutor when having a conversation, but the social contexts to which we belong or wish to belong. In Chapter 1 I have already talked about the relational and social orientation of the utterance for Bakhtin when he argues "the immediate social situation and the broader social milieu wholly determine – and determine from within, so to speak – the structure of an utterance" (Bakhtin and Volosinov, 1973, p. 86). There are two aspects to consider: one is the immediate social situation, that is to say the context in which the utterance is embedded, the other is the broader social milieu, that is to say the social landscape in which the interlocutors are immersed and which in return they contribute to shape.

In the *Discourse in the Novel* Bakhtin affirms:

in any given historical moment of verbal ideological life, each generation at each social level has its own language; moreover every age group has as a matter of fact its own language, its own vocabulary, its own particular accentual system that, in their turn, vary depending on social level, academic institution (the language of the cadet, the high school student, the trade school student are all different languages) and other stratifying factors. All this is brought up by socially typifying languages, no matter how narrow the social circle in which they are spoken.... And finally at

> any given moment, languages of various epochs and periods of socio-ideological life cohabit with one another.
>
> (Bakhtin, 1981, pp. 290–291)

Personal biography is not irrelevant in this sense and the process can never be a transparent one. As I have already quoted in the first chapter, Bakhtin affirms "a distinction can be made between two poles, two extremes between which an experience can be apprehended and ideologically structured, tending now toward the one, now toward the other". Let us label these two extremes the "I-experience" and the "we-experience". In the I-experience the more "it approaches its extreme limit, the more it loses its ideological structuredness and...also loses its verbal delineation". The "we-experience is differentiated...allows of different degrees and different types of ideological structuring" (Bakhtin and Volosinov, 1973, pp. 87–88).

Jedlowski in his book *Il sapere dell'esperienza* (1994) has studied from a sociological point of view how common sense and experience intertwine in daily life. Common sense is for Jedlowski "what people take for granted within a certain culture or a certain social circle" (Jedlowski, 1994, p. 10), while experience is "the whole of what we live everyday and of the moments that, suddenly, make us question the *sense* of all this. In other words, it is the idea of a *movement* that repeatedly takes us away from the attitude of the common sense and faces us with a personal *question of sense*" (Jedlowski, 1994, p. 11). In my research I have studied the ambivalence of storytelling acts trying to reconcile the level of the utterances with a broader sociological understanding such as that of Jedlowski, which in turn seems to me quite close to Bakhtin's approach.

Another aspect that is worth recalling at this point is that of the active and dynamic role of utterances. In Chapter 2 I have spoken about the fact that for Bakhtin the utterance is lively, is active, solves a situation, it does not merely reflect a situation, it is a situation. That, in return, influences other situations and other utterances and meaning can thus be caught only in an endless chain of signifiers and with reference to infinitive other communicative acts. The example Bakhtin employs is that of two people sitting silently in a room: "Then one of them says, 'Well!' The other does not respond" (Bakhtin and Volosinov, 1976, p. 99). I already quoted this example:

the simple word "Well!" does not only reflect a context, which is that of the snow falling in May, but rather creates a situation, which is that of the disappointment for the late snowfall. In the interviews I had with the bankers I noticed a number of these situations, where for example they say "but it's all right" or "it's fine" to express a personal answer to rather consolidated narratives: it is a personal reinscription between the "we" and the "I" in which experience emerges.

Ricoeur (1992) has used the concepts of sameness (*idem*) and self-hood (*ipse*) to describe two modes of permanence to which narrative performs the role of mediator between "the pole of character, where idem and ipse tend to coincide, and the pole of self-maintenance, where selfhood frees itself from sameness" (p. 199). And again he writes: "narrative identity oscillate between two limits: a lower limit, where permanence in time expresses the confusion of idem and ipse; and an upper limit, where the ipse poses the question of its identity without the aid and support of the idem" (Ricoeur, 1992, p. 124).

As we can see the issue is the same as that posed by Bakhtin and Jedlowski. Storytelling can express itself in different ways. What emerges from my research is the tension between these two modes. As can be seen in the next paragraph one of them is more structured that the other.

## 7.2   Consolidated narratives and rough fragments

As we have seen in Chapter 2, narrative research has aimed at studying organizational phenomena using narrative concepts. Oftentimes the work done in narrative analysis for organizational research has used the lens of the formalist/structuralist paradigm. Narrative has become a way to provide an order, a structure to an otherwise incomprehensible world.

Such interpretation does not allow, in my view, for the unpredictable, emergent and complex nature of the everyday life in organizations to be fully discovered. Experience goes beyond narratives and exceeds them. What I have learned in my research experience with the interviewed bankers is that people live their organizational life among stories; they do not live by their stories. It is only in such in-betweeness, in such ambivalence, that we can capture the essence of their experience.

Narrative research can be enriched in my view with the study of not only the social constructiveness and embeddedness of forms of determinacy but also of their precarious and emergent nature. As Boje as argued "the crisis of narrative method in modernity is what to do with nonlinear, almost living storytelling that is fragmented, polyphonic (many voiced) and collectively produced" (Boje, 2001, p. 1). His response stands in what he calls "antenarrative methods". "Stories are *antenarrative* when told without the proper plot sequence and mediated coherence preferred in narrative theory. These are stories that are too unconstructed and fragmented to be captured by retrospective sensemaking"; antenarrative "gives attention to the speculative, the ambiguity of sensemaking and guessing as to what is happening in the flow of experience" (Boje, 2001, p. 3); in antenarrative people "are still chasing stories, and many different logics for plotting an ongoing event are being investigated" (Boje, 2001, p. 4).

Antenarrative is before narrative, it is before the order and structure of retrospective interpretation. Antenarrative can be also anti narrative in the sense that it can challenge consolidated narratives. In other words, antenarrative is in the flow of experience, and it best captures the emergent and potentially subversive nature of every communicative act.

Storytelling acts, in my view, oscillate between two poles, the first is that of consolidated or structured narratives, and the second is that of rough fragments. Consolidated or structured narratives tend to be closer to the "we" mode, whereas rough fragments are closer to the "I" mode. Of course consolidated narratives are reconstructed by the subject in a personal fashion, but what is interesting there is that they are in continuous relation with collective memories, shared meanings and social identities, whereas the rough chip pole is closer to experience in the sense that Jedlowski describes it: experience "tends to emphasize the specificity of what the subject goes through, and not to take everything for granted, being typically opened to the doubt" (Jedlowski, 1994, p. 64).

Consolidated narratives and rough stories represent two poles as they never appear in pure forms in storytelling acts. I use the term consolidated here to refer to two aspects: on the one hand the fact that they are organized referring to a social "we" and presented in a unitary form; on the other hand to stress the fact that they are part of collective memory and consolidated within the community. In both cases the social "we" is dominant, as wells as the relational aspects: whereas rough fragments tend to be closer to the "I" mode where it frees itself from the societal bounds. One interesting aspect would be to analyze how the role of the interlocutor changes in organized and rough stories. Getting back to the notion of consolidated narratives, I will use the word consolidated where both aspects (coherence and reference to collective memory) are present and organized or structured stories to stress just the first aspect of them.

Storytelling acts are in the movement between these two poles and sometimes represent a third instance: that of the reinscription of one over the other as in the case of the "but it's all right" that we have seen in the previous chapters. Structured narratives refer to the objectified dimension of communication, which tends toward the absolutization of the forms of determinacy that are produced in the interactions. Determinacy is an indispensable device for social acknowledgment and it orients and structures social practices, but its reductionist character cannot fit into the complexity of experience that unexpectedly emerges in what I call rough fragments or rough stories.[6] I use the two terms interchangeably as my definition of stories is relaxed compared the beginning, middle and end notion and derives from Hannah Arendt: "Who says what is ... always tells a story, and in this story the particular facts lose their contingency and acquire some humanly comprehensible meaning" (Arendt, 1985, p. 262). I use also the word "chip" to emphasize the fact that they are fragments, but also to evoke an act of breaking and the loss of unity. The adjective "rough" on the other hand refers to the unrefined, unfinished and temporary character of this type of storytelling as in a rough copy, a first draft, but also to the nonsmooth and dissonant aspects; to the sometimes violent nature of these kind of stories, which are undisciplined and unmanageable; and finally to the coarseness and crudity of life.

If we consider the conversational storytelling that I have collected in my interviews and reported in Chapter 4 we can notice that both consolidated narratives and rough fragments are present to different degrees in the storytelling performed by the interviewees. The narratives about Frank Papen are good examples of consolidated narratives from both the bankers of the former First National Bank and Wells Fargo bank. There are some stylistic elements that I found in consolidated narratives such as Frank's narratives. One of these is the presence of refrains, whether explicitly or implicitly expressed. "Frank was not a banker" is an explicit refrain that we find in a number of the interviewees' accounts.

Let's quote again a couple of examples:

> Frank Papen, who owned the management control of the bank, he hired Charles to come in and straighten that out and so a lot of the thing that transpire during that time that Charles come to work until he got sick and he was involved in a car accident and had a tragic end, really, but he is the guy that I really credit for having saved the bank a couple of times in that process because Frank was not a banker, and the book says it and also John probably would have told you that (C1).

From another interviewee:

> in a lot of respect the executive vice-president does much more management than the president does, in some instance I know that was true when Frank Papen was the president and Charles was the executive vice-president, lot of people consider this sacrilegious to say about Frank Papen, but he was not a banker...he was a people person, he understood people and he just had the ability to gain people respect and confidence and I don't think he ever mistrusted anybody, oh that's extreme I am sure he did but he liked people (B1).

And an interview from the archives of Leon Metz:

> Frank Papen was not a banker. He didn't know banking laws and banking procedures. He was an insurance man and he knew insurance backwards and forwards. That's why he asked me to come in. He knew how to pick good people who knew banking, and therein lies his success.

In other cases such as the "Anthony story" the refrain is not as explicit as in this case, but it is implicit in the accounts, in a sort of repeated message that would sound more or less like "he was the only one that could do something like that".

Here are some examples:

One of the most interesting stories that I like to tell, I grew up in the South Valley, and I worked in Anthony, well originally when Mr Papen was putting his bank together the bank was on one side of the street and it was called First State Bank of Anthony, Texas and he bought that bank and changed the name on it to the First National Bank of Anthony and he built a huge beautiful building but what he didn't realized is that he got across the state line… Mr Haner and Mr Papen spent considerable time in Washington and they had them to change into First National Bank of Anthony, New Mexico and he changed to the First National Bank of Dona Ana county… he was the only one to ever move a bank across the state line and change the name of the bank five times (C1).

And another conversational storytelling excerpt:

(B1) John can tell you the story better and I don't know whether he did it or not, but he (Frank) acquired what was called First National Bank of Anthony, Texas.

(Linda): and he moved it across the state line…

(B1) Right and nobody know by this day how he got that done.

(Linda): and that was something he was really proud of…

(B1) I don't know whether it was a matter of power or he just confused the hell out of people and ended up with what he wanted ((LAUGHS)) I don't know, but he was able to get things done, his attitude was if it need to be done we will find a way to get it done and that was his () to go head and try.

Another consolidated narrative is that of the "Tower". The story of the construction of the tower is a narrative shared by the totality of the interviewees, and where the constant element is that of the three more floors that were not present in the initial design. Here is the reconstruction from one of the interviewees from Wells Fargo bank:

My understanding is that when they built the building it was going to be seven storey high and then Frank Papen was having a cocktail with the contractor and said what would it take to go up another three, so all the utilities, all that is on the seventh floor, where typically would be up on top, they had three more floors, that's what Ben and John have told me, the old facts (D2).

And from a former First National Bank employee:

> and originally was going to be a seven story, well he wanted a ten
> story building and they couldn't make its feasibility work and so
> they finally settle to seven and as a side the economy was in a tank
> in the late sixties and they guy that was building it had another
> job that fell through and he had a bunch of crew that he needed
> to keep busy so he went to Frank and said I'll put the other three
> story of that building for 300,000 I don't remember the number
> but significantly less it would have been had we contracted before
> because he was trying to keep his crew busy, so that's how it ended
> up to be a ten story building, if you go downtown and you go
> through that building today you would see that the air condition-
> ing and all the mechanical is on the seventh floor and that's why,
> because it was already been topped out when they came to it (C1).

The cases that I have presented here, the "Frank was not a banker", the "Anthony story" and the "Construction of the tower" are examples of shared stories that survive in the orality of Las Cruces bankers. To some degree these stories are also known outside the bank and are part of the collective memory of the community. There is a communitarian function in this type of storytelling, as well as an identity and commemorative function, according to Jedlowski's notation (2000, pp. 161–163).

What I would like to highlight here is that consolidated narratives and rough fragments are not pure forms; consolidated narratives such as the ones described may contain some rough fragments. For this reason I would rather talk about two different poles of storytelling, the one pointing toward the "we" identity, and the other being still in search, chasing meaning and sense.

Consolidated narratives and rough fragments do not coincide with these poles, but help us understand them better. It would be wrong, for example, to think that rough fragments do not hold a socialized dimension or that consolidated narratives are not shaped by personal experience of the people involved. Nevertheless we can affirm that what characterizes the pole of structured storytelling is its social dimension, its use of consolidated cognitive frames, its embeddedness in a social community.

Structured storytelling is not only the case of the consolidated narratives we have seen above, but also the case of all the storytelling fragments in which stylistic elements refer to a common cognitive structure. It is the case of the temporal development of storytelling as in one of the first extracts of Chapter 4:

> this bank was chartered in 1905 and that was even before we were a state...the...second, and before you leave you need to go up on the wall and look at all the presidents, there are pictures on the wall and the dates are up there, so if I tell you, if I miss something you go up there and verify, I think the second president of the bank was Galles and if have been here long you have heard about Lee Galles, in Albuquerque, Lee Galles, Chrysler, Chevrolet, Cadillac, all that stuff, well their grandfather was the second president of this bank; the third or the fourth president of this bank was a man named Snow, he owned all the farm you know where Stahmann Farms is on Snow Road, and he was known as the "Alfalfa king" and it's all in that book [Metz, 1991]...he was president for many years; my first recollection of the president was Mr Kelso, he was the longest running president of anybody, he was in the title company business here and I knew him for working in the bank and taking paper work on loans over to him and getting filed and put them together and they didn't write title insurances in those days, they wrote big loan scripts just describing the history of the property and guaranteeing that he didn't have or she didn't have a lain at the bank...abstract I think they call them (A1).

As already noted in Chapter 5 there are strong ties to personal and collective experience, names are connected to places that are part of collective memory, the "alfalfa king" refers to the fact that Oscar Snow had exceptional harvests with alfalfa, which he cut four or five times per years. After the first presidents the recollection jumps to personal experience, with Mr Kelso being the first president the interviewee remembers. The short description of this man's work confirms this personal experience. There is something mythical about the expression "he was the longest running president of anybody" as well as in the sentence "and it was always known as First National Bank of Las Cruces", which also reconnects personal memories with family memories. As I pointed out before, structured storytelling does not expunge personal experience aspects, as a matter of fact the socialization process can be different for each and every individual.

Along with linear development there is a set of stories that deal with the former First National bank and the business environment in which Frank Papen operated.

> Those days Las Cruces was very small he was shaking everybody's hands and you are banking with me and that's how he built up the bank (B1).

In a number of cases there is a direct reference to the past and then a jump into the present, like:

(A1)  Well, they put the plant down in Mesilla Park and they guaranteed him that they had 75 employees when they got up and running and at its peak they had 1,300 people working there.

(Boje):  13 hundred?

(A1)  Yes ((PAUSE)) and it's now shut down...

(Boje):  when did it shot down?

(A1)  Let's see what are we now? 2006? Probably it was 1992 or 1993 Stan Smith he was one of our directors he was a manager of the plant when they shot it down ((PAUSE)) they couldn't make it...but for the years they made it! ((Expression of the face))...then you know...when the market changed...so they shot that thing down and now belongs to a lumber company or something I don't know...yeah...well that was one of the many things that Mr Papen brought to Las Cruces.

As I pointed out in Chapter 5, we can see in this short conversational extract two poles of narration, on the one hand the pole of social recounting, where the bringing of business by Papen is reconstructed along with the success of the company and on the other hand the pole of experience, which may lead to the reinscription of personal experience and personal meaning to the abovementioned narrative. It is a different time and different place, also expressed in the different tone of the voice and the facial expression, the sentence "and it's now shut down" tells us more than a temporal event, offers us an opening to a dialectic that, although there is an attempt to rationalize in the following sentence "the market changed", remains at that level as a rough material.

The last sentence, "well that was one of the many things that Mr Papen brought to Las Cruces" brings us back to the socialized "we". There is a sort of cognitive structure, or pattern, which is that of "nowadays is like the way it is, but once upon a time". This is a recurrent structure in the storytelling extracts of Chapter 5.

Another good example of cognitive pattern is that of the narrative of the acquisition where Wells Fargo is recognized as a white knight saving the former First National bank from First Security Corporation. Here are some of the extracts:

> I have heard about First Security down here, Papen probably told you a little bit about that that sounded like it was a very rocky process and this was kind like a savior when Wells Fargo came in (D2).

From another interviewee:

> I don't want to use it but it was kind of the knight coming in, hey I am going to save everybody (E2).

And another:

> They (First Security Corp.) cost us half of our life…we were fortunate we had Wells Fargo to step up (A1).

This narrative is of course tied to the narrative of the rocky process of the acquisition with First Security Corporation. What is interesting noticing is that in the reconstruction of the acquisition with First Security there is a lot of rough material:

> There was a big concern about people losing their jobs and I remember asking one of the First Security people about that and they said no, nobody is going to lose their job, and that was not true (B1).

Or from another interviewee:

> And we were just very close to leave, I know I was because I had made a lot of commitment to people and I said things and made

> promises, made representation to people on how things would be, and it didn't work out that way (C1).

What I have noticed, concerning the rough material, is that there are several indicators to it. Firstly, nonverbal indicators such as pauses, drumming of the fingers, laugh and so on. Secondly, returning to the stylistic and cognitive patterns, I have noticed that rough material is often accompanied by rather unstructured stylistic patterns, such as in these last two fragments, "they said that, and it was not true" or "they made promises and it did not work that way": the conjunction "and" is significant of a loose framing and the relaxing of social determination. It is a very naturalistic device in my view, often used also by children.

It is important to say here, that the pole of rough storytelling does not always coincide with antenarrative. Antenarrative as defined by Boje (2001) is a very broad term that covers both what exists before narrative and counter-narrative. Counter-narratives can be very organized and structured as well, and follow the same patterns of narratives. My work focuses on antenarrative in the notation that excludes counter-narrative. Organizational polyphony and counter-narrative is treated, although it does not represent the core of the research. I have shown in Chapter 5 the different voices, and insisted on the different reconstructions made by the former managing team of First National bank and that of Wells Fargo, but the interviews used for this work are the interviews of bankers that are, or were, in very high positions within the bank and interestingly all males. I did interview former employees of Wells Fargo bank but I decided not to include those extracts in the book. Of course those extracts would show organizational polyphony and counter-narratives on a higher level.

Returning to the two poles of storytelling one interesting aspect that I have already pointed out is that of the third time, which is kind of movement between the first and the second pole as witnessed in storytelling fragments:

> We don't make any big loan decision here, we don't make any investment decision here, we do make some personnel decision based on company policies, you know, but they are not life chang-ing decisions, if they got a three million loan and they want to

make it and everybody here is behind it and then they sent it to
the next level and if they don't like it it's not going to happen
but that's all right too, you have to have everything in place, it's a
different philosophy (A1).

The "but that's all right too", is precisely this third time, the signaling
of the movement between the two. I think that in this third time we
can find the power of stories, and their appeal. As Marquard puts it:
"the truth is one thing, but the way we can live with the truth is
another. Knowledge serves the former, cognitively and stories serve
the latter, vitally... their task [stories] is not to find the truth, but to
find a modus vivendi with truth" (Marquard, 1989, p. 90).

Storytelling, as said before in the fifth chapter, has a lot to do with
coping with pain, with a soothing function as described by Gabriel.

Again another example of this:

Looking back at that right now and the way they do things, it was
completely... I am sure small banks are still run that way today to
a certain degree, but... I don't know. I have never been in their
decision-making process, in today's world, I have no decision-
making and that is what is hard for me to EXIST with because
I was so used of making them and so was Tom and Ben. I don't
have any authority to do anything, I can't... which is fine... it's
all right, it's just different, it's just a different life. YOU KIND OF
MISS NOT MAKING DECISIONS (A1).

As we may notice "you kind of" is the an expression of experience,
while "I don't know" would be closer to Jedlowski, suspension of a
doubt and represent an antenarrative reference in Boje's terms. "It's
all right" expresses what I label third time of narration.

And here is the extract that I consider one of the best examples
of this:

I will never forget the day we were all at the double eagle restaurant
and ((goes and picks up a clock on the shelf))... gave me this clock
February second 1998,... It was a marvelous time in my life and
I thought I was rich, but I wasn't... but that's all right (A1).

Rough stories and the movement between the two poles seem to have the function of reminding us about the complexity of life, and having to cope with it. Both rough stories and consolidated narratives on the other hand have to do with a sort of a landscape that is probably typical of a culture, or a place or a generation.

I have often wondered if there are subjects that are more prone to the rough storytelling, and from a first glance we can see that there are more rough fragments in the accounts of the bankers of the former First National Bank of Dona Ana, but we have to consider that there is a factor that cannot be neglected: the bankers of First National tell First National now, it is an account of the past made in the present, while the Wells Fargo bankers tell Wells Fargo in the same moment, it is an account of the present made in the present. One explication could be the importance of context: put in a different context people gain experience of their stories.

An interesting triangulation I have made is that of using a lot of references from the book of Leon Metz. The accounts of First National are made at the same time in which they were narrated, and as a matter of fact present less rough fragments. But it may be argued that that is also a different type of storytelling because it is written and is not spontaneous conversational storytelling.

Another interesting research path would be that of studying both consolidated and rough stories in their relation to narrative models that are typical of certain cultures. My guess is that consolidated narratives follow specific cultural modules, while rough stories represent alternatives, or elements that cannot fit in the paradigm. In this case they remain at a rough level and can eventually become narrative themselves. The interesting aspect is that their presence or the acknowledgment of their presence for the individual can be a source of unease, if not panic, or can lead to positive reconstruction as in the case of the "it's all right" of our bankers. This third time is also shaped by cultural modules and as a matter of fact the "it's all right" module is common to most of the former First National bankers.


## 7.3   Myths and storytelling

Along with the study of storytelling acts, together with Professor Boje I carried out a study on myth in Las Cruces banking that has been recently published (Boje and Musacchio, 2008). In this study I have studied the Wells Fargo myth in Las Cruces using the narrative/antenarrative method and the ideas of consolidated versus rough stories. In particular I have studied the intertwining of written and codified stories reconstructing a mythology of the south west and of the orality of the storytelling performed among the bankers community. Written and encoded mythologies are expressed in Wells Fargo logo: the stagecoaches, shown in Figure 7.1. Being in the south-west, the logo is highly significative. It has to do with the myth of the South-West.

However, the story of Wells Fargo bank now has little to do with the old Wells Fargo freight business of the pioneers. As a matter of fact, and without giving justice to the complexity of the mergers up to that point, Wells Fargo had been acquired in 1998 by Norwest who, capitalizing on its long history and the famous trademark stagecoach logo, changed its name to Wells Fargo & Company. Headquarters were moved to the San Francisco base of Wells Fargo, while Richard Kovacevich, former head of Norwest became president and CEO of the newly formed bank. Coming from the Norwest

*Figure 7.1*   The logo of the bank in one of the branches. (Picture taken by Marisa Ortman.)

tradition, Kovacevich was a recognized leader in the financial service industry and the one associated with the store, sales-people culture and with cross-selling strategy (Wikipedia, Richard Kovacevich, 2007). One question could be whether this was the same bank, before and after the depression up to 1983 and to the 1998 merger.

Now, this story merges with the over 2,000 banks that Wells Fargo had bought since then (Wikipedia, Wells Fargo, 2007). There is an interesting interplay between the orality, the visuality and the textuality in the case studied. In the orality we can retrace elements that are erased in the textuality and visuality. An example of the erasure in textuality is the brochure I mentioned in Chapter 5, shown in Figure 7.2.

*Figure 7.2*   Wells Fargo brochure.

In 1998, Wells Fargo and Norwest joined in a merger of equals. Then at the beginning of this new century, Wells Fargo acquired First National Bank of Farmington and First Security offices in the greater metropolitan area of Albuquerque, Las Cruces, Roswell and Santa Fe. The heritage of these pioneer New Mexico financial institutions lives under the familiar Wells Fargo name.

With regard to visuality, if one walks along Main Street, in Las Cruces, New Mexico one will see a big building and on top of the building the name Wells Fargo. Not only did that building become Wells Fargo a few years ago, but it can also be argued that the building is the exact expression of the First National Bank mythology. In the visuality there are no traces of this past: but if we talk with executives of Wells Fargo Bank we hear the stories that I have reported both in this chapter and in Chapter 5. Wells Fargo mythology although superimposed in the visuality cannot suppress preexisting mythologies such as the stories of the tower that are recounted by all the interviewed bankers, both from the old community and the new.

What emerges from the case is a problematization of the mnemonic function of storytelling and the importance of storytelling in the survival of a plurality of myths. As Marquard warns us: "Dangerous is the destiny of the one who will live monomythically one story – as fascinated by the new myth of the sole history, one sticks to the path that is only supposedly the path to heaven on earth and is in reality the path to identity, on earth, of heaven and hell: to an integrated, all purpose identity" (Marquard, 1989, p. 103).

# 8
# Models of Decision-Making and the Everydayness of Decisions

This chapter on decision-making reflects my initial interest on the relation between decision-making and narrating practices. As already discussed in Chapter 2 in the section on narrative and decision-making, the core of the research has changed over the years as the result of both epistemological and pragmatic considerations. At this point to come back to the theme of decision-making is more for the respect of the initial commitment that a necessity; however some of the interviews of Chapter 5 can be read in the light of that interest, rather than making any conclusion on the subject they can be seen as suggestions for further researches on the topic. In this chapter I will review models of decision-making as scholars belonging to very different realms have theorized them. A discourse on storytelling might seem out of place in this context, however what I would like to show is that storytelling can be a complement if not an alternative to such paradigm. Storytelling represents a way of engaging in research but also, in my view, can lead to new models of theory of action; a shift from the cognitive understanding to a more "corporeal" understanding of such phenomena.

Every day CEOs and top managers of corporate companies and banking institutions make strategic decisions. Scholars belonging to the economic and managerial field have theorized such decisions using alternative paradigms ranging from normative to descriptive accounts. Among the descriptive accounts in the last section I will focus on an understanding of decision-making from within, in terms of the experience of people involved in these processes, by showing extracts of interviews with bankers talking about decision-making practices. I say corporeal understanding of decision-making practices, because I believe that by reading such storytelling fragments we get closer to the "who" of decisions instead of the "what" and "how" of the models. Memories, experiences and socialized accounts, become the focus of the research: the daily landscape of work life.

Narrative/antenarrative research helps us to get closer to the world of the bankers involved in the decision-making processes, to their collective view of decisions and to their personal distance from them, moreover, narrative/antenarrative research helps us to feel closer to the coping mechanisms of bankers regarding decisions.

Bankers in the interviews never talk about decision-making in a formal and abstract way, they relate decision-making practices to their personal work life experience, to the everyday practices of their work, to the role of Frank, the patriarch. They talk about choices, consequences and costs while telling us stories about the bank and about themselves.

## 8.1　Models of decision-making: Normative and descriptive approaches

Decision-making processes have been studied, over time, in different epistemic traditions and disciplines. One common distinction is made between individual and organizational decision-making. In this chapter I will not follow such a distinction but rather present approaches developed in both senses. I have found it relevant to present both approaches for several reasons. The reason for including individual behavioral decision theory lies mainly in the fact that behavioral decision theory shares the same roots (I am referring to Herbert Simon's notion of procedural rationality) as many critical underpinnings of organizational decision-making, calling for a revision of the normative statistical decision theory model. Secondly, the very idea of rational decision is tied to the economic neoclassical notion of subjective utility maximization. Moreover organizations, until the seminal works of Cyert and March (1963) and March and Simon (1958), were seen as purely economic functions and no attention was paid to the structural aspects of decision-making. It is therefore relevant, in my view, to consider an approach that has within the economic paradigm itself questioned some of the assumptions of the normative models and acknowledged the formation of heuristics and biases in judgment as well as in the choice behavior of the individuals.

On the other hand organizational decision-making theories have dealt with the contextual aspects of decision-making processes such as the relation between means and ends (Cohen, March and Olsen, 1972; Lindblom, 1959); sense-making (Weick, 1994); negotiation (Allison, 1969); power and environmental dependency (Pfeffer, 1981; Salancik, 1977), just to name a few of them.

It is interesting to notice that the roots of the management field, and in particular organizational studies, lie in the study of social behavior, and as a matter of fact the seminal work of Simon was called *Administrative Behavior* (1947). The approach used in this research goes back to such roots of organizational understanding, far from the grandiosity (Alvesson, 2007) of some discourses on decision-making and elaborated algorithms, by studying the decision makers, in a naturalistic way, in their daily work in organizations. It will seem to the reader that decision-making will slowly disappear along with the development of the work, but this is not true. A different perspective will be demonstrated on the subject of decision-making that will not be treated as a topic per se but rather as a part of the daily life of managers in banking institutions.

### 8.1.1   Rational actor model

In the economics and management fields the idea of pure rational decision-making has represented a paradigm that still holds for its normative appeal. Decision-making theory in such domains has been dominated by Bayesian decision theory which argues for the maximization of subjective expected utility.

> Its elegance [Bayesian decision theory] retains a hold on the imagination of scholars, and its familiarity makes it a reference point to which other theories must relate. Any general account of decision making must define itself relative to Bayesian decision theory. Any such account must explain why it does not do things that Bayesian decision theory does, or why it does some things differently.
>
> (Shafer, 1990)

Expected utility theory (von Neumann and Morgenstern, 1944; Savage, 1954) dates back to the work of Bernoulli in 1738 and to the more recent work of John von Neumann and Oskar Morgenstern (1944) on game theory, as well as that of Abraham Wald (1939) on statistical decision theory, popularized by Raiffa et al. (Luce and Raiffa, 1957; Pratt, Raiffa and Schlaifer, 1965).

The normative model drawn by such works is known as the rational actor model and portrays decision-making as an essentially orderly and rational process where a problem is defined and isolated, information is gathered, alternatives are identified, and an end is established. Goals, values or objectives that guide the decision maker are clarified and ranked according to their importance in utility terms. Consequences (costs and benefits, advantages and disadvantages) that flow from each alternative are investigated and compared on a same scale. According to such models the decision maker is able to choose the alternative that maximizes the attainment of his or her goals, values or objective. It is an "intentional, consequential and optimizing" process (March, 1988, p. 1). Once the decision problem is defined and objectives are clear, alternatives are searched and evaluated, choice is made and implementation will follow.

In the management field this approach has been operationalized by the so called cost-benefits analysis. In this case a decision is considered worthwhile for the management when the value of the benefits of a course of action is higher than the costs associated with it. The paradigm is again that of the rational actor who chooses between the possible options, which are all known to him and comparable numerically, by the means of a probability measure or thanks to the reduction of the costs-benefits to a common unit of measure (money).

This means-ends paradigm subtends the type of rationality that James March defines as "intentional and consequential" as the economic agent anticipates the consequences of his actions on the basis of linear cause-effect relationships and retains his discretionality in the way that would maximize the achievement of the specific goal (and not about which kind of goal should be preferable).

Once alternatives are set and possible actions are explored, consequences are driven and evaluated, and decision rule is chosen, choice will follow (March, 1994). This kind of rationality is also known as comprehensive rationality and posits for a clear distinction between the ends to be attained, a perfect knowledge of the alternatives and the possibility of computing the outcomes of the consequences for each alternative.

Such a model holds its appeal thanks to the fact that it eliminates uncertainty (as not structurally included in the model) and serves for control of the environment as a safety device. Similarly, in the strategic management domain an unrivaled positivistic rational orientation (Chandler, 1962; Porter, 1979; Taylor 1947) has ruled for years, seeking its justification in the need for eliminating and incorporating uncertainty and chaos, and coordinating activities. The idea was that of structure following strategy from the famous "Unless structure follows strategy, inefficiency rules" (Chandler, 1962, p. 314).

### 8.1.2  Bounded rationality

Different orientations have taken into account the complexity of the conditions that can affect the utility optimization process. Bounded rationality models have taken into consideration limited time, information and resources in dealing with complex and multidimensional issues (March, 1978; Simon, 1957).

According to bounded rationality scholars decisions never occur in a predictable environment in which full information is provided, decision makers are alone and preferences are fixed. On the contrary decisions are taken by people who belong to organizations, in an environment that is often unpredictable, where objectives are often confused and get discovered only when proceeding into action, and where information is bounded to the available resources.

The process as normatively prescribed under the rational model is questioned from a descriptive point of view. Already the definition of alternatives within organizational contexts becomes problematic. Alternatives are not just there, nor are they defined by organizations as a "collective mind" but rather are the result of an interaction between the individuals that, for Cyert and March (1963), takes the form of coalition. Of course there is a subjective utility calculation behind it but the stress is on the fact that organizations cannot be taken as single entities. From this derives that individual subjective utility may differ from one individual to another leading to infinitive configurations. Some individuals may be interested in monetary payoffs while others may be driven by power and prestige issues, other than professional and career development, and so on. Even in a stable group such as that of the bankers of the First National bank we see that each of the main decision makers had different views and approaches to the decision-making practice. Moreover, agreements on the alternatives are often formulated in a confused and ambiguous way, as ambiguity is often the necessary condition for reaching agreement; such alternatives are often conflicting and get discovered only along the way.

Another question is that of perfect information, or omniscience, as one of the main assumptions of the neoclassical economic vision. The Arrow-Debreu general-equilibrium theory is the best-known example of this, in which highly simplified agents are required to know all the utilities and production possibilities of all other agents. This is of course costly and thus influenced by budget constraints. Classical theory states that there is a gain in obtaining all the information, as information is worthwhile up to the point that the marginal cost of searching for more information is equal to the marginal utility.

Feldman and March (1981) have shown that "information is not gathered as the classical decision theory posits because it helps to make a choice nor investment in information are made up to the point at which marginal expected cost equals marginal expected return" rather "they gather information and do not use it. They ask for reports and do not read them. They act first and receive requested information later" (Feldman and March, 1981, p. 182). Of course this is not senseless; Feldman and March argue that information, although not used for decision, is gathered for control and surveillance purposes, symbolic (shows commitment to rational choice) and social (signals personal and organizational competence) purposes. The bounded rationality model shows also that the way in which information is available influences judgment as we will see in the section on behavioral decision theory.

Finally, reflections are made also on the selection of alternatives. Within organizations there are repertoires of choices that are already available. This can be an obstacle to new configurations and may reduce the set of possible alternatives. According to these critiques bounded rationality scholars view decision-making processes more as a "satisficing" (Simon, 1957) than an optimizing process and this is because decision makers are constrained by limited cognitive capabilities and incomplete information (March and Simon, 1958). "Most human decision-making, whether individual or organizational, is concerned with the discovery and selection of satisfactory alternatives; only in exceptional cases is it concerned with the discovery and selection of optimal alternatives" (March and Simon, 1958, p. 162).

As we can see the normative rational model is not completely rejected but rather enriched with more descriptive realism. Very original in this endeavor is the analysis of Graham Allison in his book *The Essence of Decision: Explaining the Cuban Missile Crisis* (Allison, 1969) whose title is based on a speech by John F. Kennedy, in which he said "The essence of ultimate decision remains impenetrable to the observer – often, indeed, to the decider himself". As in Kurosawa *Rashomon* (1950), where the same story is recounted by three different characters with three different understandings, Allison (1969) provides three different levels of analysis for the Cuban missile crisis; the first level being the rational actor model, the second the organizational one and the third the political one.

Allison can be associated with the bounded rationality tradition as he contended in his book that nations consider all options and act rationally to maximize their utility when making decisions: but its relevance for this study is also in the fact that he approaches the decision-making process from different angles and using a different lens. Every point of view has its own legitimation and explicatory power and the three different perspectives contribute to the creation of an understanding of the decision process. It is also interesting from a research design point of view as, instead of analyzing the same phenomenon in different decision settings, Allison concentrates on one single episode (the Cuban missile crisis) and on different interpretations of it.

According to the first level, governments are seen as individuals who are able to maximize utility. It is a simple heuristic device to consider agents in this way, Allison argues, and sometimes the easiest one when we do not dispose of a great diversity of sources. At the organizational level, he argued (according to March and Simon's bounded rationality) that government's leaders are faced with limited resources and often follow already set repertoires when taking actions. But even this understanding is not satisfactory for Allison who argues also for a third level of analysis, which is to say the political one.

Following this level of analysis he stated that nation's actions can be interpreted only with reference to the negotiation that takes place at the top governmental level and are driven by the personal interests involved. Players according to Allison "pull and haul" over the political choices. Decisions are thus the results of these multiple and simultaneous games and for this reason every analysis of decision-making processes should detect who the players are in the game, what their objectives are, their influence on final decisions, what the stakes are and the rules of the game.

### 8.1.3   Behavioral decision theory

As stated before I will introduce some key aspects of behavioral decision theory as this field has provided (and is still providing) descriptively realistic accounts of judgment and choice following the line of some of the critiques included in Herbert Simon's notion of procedural and bounded rationality, and in particular the cognitive constraint individuals face when assessing probabilities and selecting between alternatives. These aspects are not treated in my empirical research, which has a different focus, but I think they are extremely relevant as their purpose is that of "increasing the explanatory power of economic models by providing it with more realistic psychological foundations" (Camerer, Loewenstein and Rabin, 2004, p. 3).

Again the neoclassical approach is not rejected completely but some of its assumptions are revised and tested. It is work done mainly by economists and cognitive psychologists in laboratories aiming at analyzing in detail the ways in which individuals deviate from Bayesian decision theory in their judgment and choices. Important results were acquired in the field and it is nowadays clear, thanks to these experiments, that such deviations are substantial. People do not use subjective expected utility to make the majority of their everyday decisions, and often their choices cannot be reconciled with any ranking by subjective expected utility.

Behavioral economic scholars have shown individuals' limited ability to process information and the systematic biases and simplifying decision procedures that people employ (Kleindorfer, Kunreuther and Shoemaker, 1993, p. 5). The study of discrepancies between the rational actor theory and the considered behavior of economic agents has generated a well documented set of systematic errors or biases that individuals make when making decisions. Experiments conducted (Kahneman and Tversky, 1979; Kahneman, Slovic and Tversky, 1982) have shown that utility functions are not linear (Allais

1953; Ellsberg, 1961), preferences are not stable (Kahneman and Tversky, 1979; Thaler 1980) and they vary substantially according to the way in which the choice problem is presented, "framed" (Kahneman and Tversky, 1979; Kahneman, Slovic and Tversky 1982).

There are two main streams of research in behavioral decision theory: one deals with judgment and the other with choice. In the first case research deals with the simplification procedures people employ when estimating probabilities or when selecting between alternatives in the second case.

When estimating probabilities, likelihood is related to "statistical sampling and Bayes' rule for updating probabilities in the face of new evidence" (Camerer, Loewenstein and Rabin, 2004, p. 9). Empirical evidence has shown that this is cognitively unrealistic because it "requires a separation between previously judged probabilities and evaluations of new evidence... [while] many cognitive mechanisms use previous information to filter or interpret what is observed, violating this separability" also "subjective expected utility assumes separability between probability judgements of states and utilities that result from this states (wishful thinking)" and finally "order of arrival of information distorts probability judgment" (Camerer, Loewenstein and Rabin, 2004, pp. 9–10).

In their seminal work *Judgment under uncertainty: Heuristics and Biases*, Kahneman, Slovic and Tversky (1982) show that "people rely on a limited number of heuristic principles which reduce the complex tasks of assessing probabilities and predicting values to simpler judgmental operations. In general, these heuristics are quite useful, but sometimes they lead to severe and systematic errors" (Tversky and Kahneman, 1974, p. 1124). Some examples of this are availability heuristics, representativeness and confirmation bias, just to name a few.

According to the availability heuristic, people assess the frequency, probability or likely causes of an event by the degree to which instances or occurrences of that event are readily available in their memory. Representativeness heuristic shows that "we think a person to be a member of a group if he is similar to the typical member of that group... Research on the representativeness heuristic, demonstrates that people tend to over-use representativeness in assessing probabilities" (Kahneman, Slovic and Tversky, 1982, p. 156). Under the confirmation bias people are less attentive to relevant new information supporting or contradicting their hypothesis once forming strong hypothesis.

Other heuristics I will just mention without entering in to detail for brevity reasons are adjustment and anchoring biases, hindsight bias, law of small numbers and the gambler's fallacy (over infer from short sequences). For a detailed description of such heuristics see Baron (1988, pp. 224–238).

On the other hand behavioral decision theory has dealt with short-cuts made by individuals when choosing between alternatives and questioned whether they are reference independent (that is to say they are not affected by individual reference level) and invariant to variations in the way options are described.

Framing bias (Kahneman, Slovic and Tversky, 1982) arises when trivial changes to the way a decision problem is presented lead to different choices. Two logically equivalent statements framed in a different way, emphasizing either the potential gains or potential losses, lead to reversals of preference, with decision-makers being risk averse when gains are highlighted and risk seeking when losses are highlighted. Preferences are shown to be labile rather than fixed and they are constructed in the elicitation procedure.

This has been elaborated in the so called "Prospect Theory" (Tversky and Kahneman, 1992) which is an economic model (different from descriptive indications of bounded rationality) in which the valuation of outcomes has a particular shape, which differs consistently whether we are in the losses or gains relative to a reference point (for simplification purposes it can be considered as status quo wealth). The function is concave for gains and convex for losses and it is steeper in the domain of losses. This is due to "diminishing sensitivity", that is to say the marginal change in perceived well-being is greater for changes that are close to one's reference level than for changes that are further away, and to "loss aversion", which states that losses are weighted more that commensurate gains, as shown in Table 8.1.

Other experiments have also dealt with the self-interest assumption made in classical economics. The very theorists of this model were actually more concerned with psychological aspects than the later neoclassical ones who expunged psychology from economics.

*Table 8.1*   From Rabin, 1998.

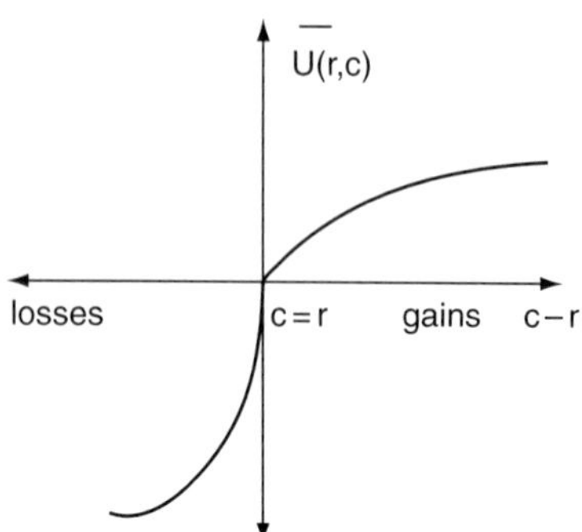


As a matter of fact, Adam Smith wrote "it is not from the benevolence of the butcher, the brewer, or the baker that we expect our dinner, but from their regard to their own interest" (Smith, 1776) and in his *Theory of Moral Sentiments* (Smith, 1759) he has deeply analyzed human behavior and the socializing process that sustains it. Behavioral economists have questioned the assumption of self-interest showing that "people may sometimes choose to spend their wealth to punish others who have harmed them, reward those who have helped, or make outcomes fairer" (Camerer, Loewenstein and Rabin, 2004, p. 27). It is the case of the "ultimatum game", or other trust game experiments (Güth and Thiez, 1990; Thaler, 1988), studying gain seeking behavior of economic agents focusing on fairness and reciprocity behavior (Fehr and Gachter, 2000).

### 8.1.4   Garbage can model and the science of muddling through

If in the last paragraphs the limits to the rational model emerged at an individual level, these paragraphs concentrate on the overall irrational behavior of organizations when dealing with decision problems. Again some of the assumptions of the rational model are questioned and among them the strict causality between problems and choices, where first problems are identified, then choices are made. According to the Garbage can model (Cohen, March and Olsen, 1972) and the muddling though model of Lindblom (1959) there are many situations in organizations where such logical sequence is not followed.

Problematic preference is a property of the organized anarchies described by the garbage can model. "The organization operates on the basis of a variety of inconsistent and ill-defined preferences. It can be described better as a loose collection of ideas than as a coherent structure; it discovers preferences through action more than it acts on the basis of preferences" (Cohen, March and Olsen, 1972, p. 1) and again "participants arrive at an interpretation of what they are doing and what they have done while in the process of doing it. From this point of view, an organization is a collection of choices looking for problems, issues and feelings looking for decision situations in which they might be aired, solutions looking for issues to which they might be the answer, and decision makers looking for work" (Cohen, March, and Olsen, 1972, p. 2).

Together with problematic preferences, unclear technology and fluid participation is shown. Organizations make decisions on the basis of trial and error procedures, learning from past experience and following pragmatic intuition, and the amount of time and effort devoted to different decisions may change according to interest and commitment.

Based on the above, Cohen, March and Olsen use the metaphor of the garbage can:

> one can view a choice opportunity as a garbage can into which various kinds of problems and solutions are dumped by participants as they are generated. The mix of garbage in a single can depends on the mix of cans available, on the labels attached to the alternative cans, on what garbage is currently being produced, and on the speed with which garbage is collected and removed from the scene … in a garbage can model a decision is an outcome or interpretation of several relatively independent streams within an organization.
>
> (Cohen, March, and Olsen, 1972, pp. 2–3)

The striking innovation here is to capture decision-making as processes in which problems and solutions are not consequential or sometimes even reversed in their order of appearance, in which participants come and go and choice opportunities are "occasions when an organization is expected to produce behavior that can be called a decision" (Cohen, March and Olsen, 1972, p. 3). The streams of solutions, problems, choice opportunities and participants are considered as autonomous streams that cross the organization and eventually meet in what we call the decision. The metaphor of the garbage emphasizes the randomness of throwing an object into the can.

The authors found that three different decision styles emerged in their study of university administrations: the first is oversight, where choice is made "without any attention to existing problems and with a minimum of time and energy" (Cohen, March and Olsen, 1972, p. 8); the second is flight, where participants and solutions tend to fly together from choice to choice; and finally resolution often associated with unimportant choices.

> It is also recognized that, even if people know what they want, they do not always behave consistently with their objectives because of organizational procedures, weakness of will, or by retrospectively establishing goals that rationalize decisions already made. A purely rational organizational design that ignores this is not merely false but may be the cause of misadaptation and ineffectiveness in bureaucratic organizations. It is important to distinguish formal and informal organizational structures in that, disproportionate emphasis on formal procedures (e.g. charts, rules, and management techniques) does not eradicate but instead shifts uncertainty to new areas of unpredictability and negotiation.
>
> (Warglien and Masuch, 1996)

I would add here the pioneering work of Lindblom (1959) who problematized the causality and separability of mean ends (as described in the rational comprehensive model) in public administration settings. In his article he refers to decision processes as the "Science of Muddling Trough" (Lindblom, 1959) and proposes a "successive limited comparisons" model where policy makers and administrators tend to build on existing policies, slightly changing them through incrementally "muddling through".

He compares what he calls the "branch method (successive limited comparisons) [ ] continually building out from the current situation, step by step and by small degrees" and the "root method (rational-comprehensive) [ ] starting from fundamentals anew each time, building on the past only as experience is embodied in a theory, and always prepared to start completely from the ground up" (Lindblom, 1959, p. 241). Keeping in mind the powerful suggestion of the succession of comparisons as the result of the study "policy is not made once and for all; it is made and remade endlessly" (Lindblom, 1959, p. 250) and the substitution of theory (root method) by comparative analysis (branch method) – "administrators know that the available theory will work less well than more modest incremental comparisons" (Lindblom, 1959, p. 250); I will concentrate on the first two assumptions of the model, that is to say the nonseparability of value and goals, and of means and ends.

For Lindblom, values and goals are not distinct from one another, but are closely intertwined. "The idea that values should be clarified, and in advance of the examination of alternative policies, is appealing. But what happens when we attempt it for complex social problems? [ ] on many critical values or objectives citizens disagree, congressmen disagree and public administrations disagree [ ] by the impossibility of doing otherwise, administrators often are reduced to deciding policy without clarifying objectives first" (Lindblom, 1959, pp. 242–243). He then goes on to argue that values are often conflicting even for a single administrator and social objectives do not always have the same relative values. For these reasons "one chooses among values and among policies at one and the same time" (Lindblom, 1959, p. 244).

It follows also that means and ends are not distinct, as they are simultaneously chosen. Of course this can be regarded as nonsense for many, as "how can an administrator know whether he has made a wise or foolish decision if he is without prior values or objectives by which to judge his decisions?" (Lindblom, 1959, p. 245). But this calls on another aspect, which is how to judge a decision. This is a far more complex matter to which Lindblom answers that there is no standard of correctness and solution for the agreement on the policy itself. We will see later on how this complex issue is solved for authors in a similar direction questioning the validity of objectives themselves, if not appropriate for the social culture in which they are performed. Both the garbage can model and the science of muddling through are powerful descriptive models of the everyday lives of decision makers. In the extracts of the interviews with the community bankers you will see that the decision-making processes described are rather informal where it is difficult to clearly distinguish the moment of choices which emerge in a continuum of social interactions among bankers.

### 8.1.5  Problematizing the concept of decision

It is in this direction that we can read the second wave of work from Henry Mintzberg (compared to the work done in the seventies were he analyzed decision processes in a rather objective fashion) in his discussion article with Waters, Pettigrew and Butler. Mintzberg and Waters argued against the causality between commitment and actions and in their brilliant study they actually come to realize that such a separation can be misleading in the studying of organizations as decisions "don't exist, in other words, that the relationship between decision and action can be far more tenuous than almost all literature of organization theory suggests" (Mintzberg and Waters, 1990, p. 2).

It is not possible to distinguish between decision and actions, and every attempt to study decisions as a distinct entity will lead to failure. It is very difficult to locate the very moment of a decision and sometimes not even the persons involved in the process are able to come to a solution. Sometimes the origin of a decision can be traced back to a moment that we cannot even relate to the decision. The case of the coffee shop from our interviewees is significant in this sense.

Moreover, as argued by Mintzberg and Waters, sometimes actions are performed without traceable formal decisions and this is not only at an individual but also at an organizational level. It is, for example, the case of the General Motors manager who describes a committee in which somebody sums up the emerging position and all the others are nodding, the example made by Mintzberg and Waters in their article.

Here is what one of the community bankers interviewed said:

> We all knew, when we went to a meeting we knew what we were going to talk about, the one in charge of that particular area carried the conversation and we basically said yes or no (A1).

The idea is that commitment does not always precede action; it can be ambiguous or sometimes nonexistent. Organizations, as well as bureaucracies sometimes need formal procedures for decision-making. Here we enter in a different subject, that is how people cope with such formal requirements and what these requirements mean for their experience of decisions.

What can be retained of Mintzberg and Water's argument is that the definition itself of decision is quite problematic as in organizational settings it is often hard to locate exactly when decisions are made and by whom. Instead of a linear and clearly defined process, decision-making is more an elaborated, continuously reshaped and redefined process and for this reason Pettigrew (1990) insists on the notion of change rather than decision as the focus of analysis. In his extensive research on organizations Pettigrew has focused his attention on long-term strategies rather than single decision moments with a special emphasis on the context in which these strategies were performed and how these were perceived within the organizations by its members.

### 8.1.6   Sense-making

Weick's contribution to decision-making processes is quite unique in the sense that he postulates that organizing and making sense of reality share the same roots. Here the question is not about the consequentiality of action and decision as they are both results of sense-making, an ex-post process which gives meaning to experience. The focus is on the way people involved in organizing make sense of the events happening around them. Decision makers (or rather people belonging to organizations) are seen as active and conscious agents capable of organizing discrepant and often implausible events.

It is a different process from interpretation, as Weick himself argues: "Most descriptions of interpretation focus on some kind of text. What sensemaking does is address how the text is constructed as well how it is read. Sensemaking is about authoring as well as reading" (Weick, 1994, p. 7) and again "the key distinction is that sensemaking is about the ways people generate what they interpret" (Weick, 1994, p. 13). And this is where construction takes place.

Narratives can represent a way to make sense of a situation. In Chapter 2 I have presented the work carried out by Orr (1990) on the role of narrative in problem solving. Orr describes two clerks repairing copiers that present error codes that are not plausible and how they solved the situation by telling each other stories of similar situations that had happened in the past. It is a process of fitting, or framing new (novel) circumstances into structures of understanding or schemas. We may notice that this perspective envisions stories as prescriptive devices that can be activated when ambiguity or uncertainty reigns.

Sense-making applied to decision-making shifts attention from the way people make decisions to the mechanisms by which people make sense of the problem on which they will then decide. Once sense-making is achieved, decisions will follow.

One of the main themes in Weick's previous work (Weick, 1969) is found in the recipe "How can I know what I think until I see what I say?" quoted from Wallas (1926, p. 106), which revitalizes the old puzzle of the relationship between thought, experience and language. According to Weick's interpretation, the enactment of a social reality is the central process according to which people find out what they are saying and retrospectively understand what they think.

Of course this has manifold consequences on the description of decision-making processes; how do people in organizations agree on such enactment? How is enactment made visible? Do people adhere to certain rules when making sense of reality? What are these rules or patterns, and so on.

One important aspect to mention here is that Weick's constructionist view of organizations' sense-making neglects one very critical issue: power. For this reason for social constructionist aspects I will refer to the work of Berger and Luckmann (1966), which is in my view much more fitting in a sociological discourse on organizations.

In the empirical research performed I have collected examples of very different sense-making processes carried out within the same organization: personal negotiation, superimposition and conflict are just some of the possible endings. For this reason I find it difficult to talk about collective sense-making processes without referring to the constant negotiation going on, both on a personal and organizational level. Boje's notions of the storytelling organization (1991) and antenarrative (2001) address exactly this issue.

## 8.2   The everydayness of decision

In this section I will outline a proposal for research that takes into account the experience of the people involved in the decision-making processes themselves. This approach does not undervalue the normative and descriptive models abovementioned, but it proposes a different lens of analysis for the decision-making process.

March (1997) distinguishes between decisions as rational choices and decisions as rule-base actions.

> In particular it has been argued that theories of rational, anticipatory, calculated, consequential action underestimate both the pervasiveness and intelligence of an alternative decision logic – the logic of appropriateness, obligation, duty and rules…actual decisions in organizations, as in individuals, seem often to involve finding appropriate rules to follow…rather than evaluating alternatives in terms of the values of their consequences, it matches situations and identities…actions reflect images of proper behavior.
>
> (March, 1997, p. 17)

March's argument seems to fit with what one of the interviewees said:

> Lot of the management decisions were based on the vision of the individual manager and the actual practice in my view was more a function of what appeared to be prudent and sound based on common sense as opposed to meeting any defined criteria (B1).

However, common sense is a social construction to which people may dissent:

> And when we were at meeting for a specific individual that has been working for the bank for some period of time and Frank Papen said "no, that person has been with us for a long time", we would keep that person (B1).

As well as having input into decision-making, sense-making is also an output of it, as in the case of Frank Papen's decisions. As we have seen in Chapter 5, in the case of Frank Papen decision and identity would go hand in hand, and everybody would be able to tell you what Frank would have liked or not.

Decision-making as envisioned in the rational model posits the fact that people make choices based on the utility maximization scheme, and thus we can ask ourselves whether they are choices at all. March, citing Duesenberry, says that "economics is all about how people make choices; sociology is all about how they don't have any choice to make" and then states that "students of organizational decisions locate themselves happily in the midst of the distinction" (March, 1997, p. 9). This is an extremely powerful suggestion that needs in my view to be problematized.

Social scientists have argued that socializing processes sustains every economic action (as we have seen argued already by Smith) and have described the social embeddedness of economic action "actors do not behave or decide as atoms outside a social context, nor [do] they adhere slavishly to a script written for them by the particular intersection of social categories that they happen to occupy. Their attempts at purposive action are instead embedded in concrete, ongoing systems of social relations" (Granovetter, 1985).

The narrative/antenarrative lens helps us frame the continuous conflict between socially constructed and mediated rules and personal positioning toward them, in a continuum that is sometime hardly distinguishable. There are cases in which alternatives are created as in this case from the same example as above:

> But I got a little more aggressive one year, I felt if somebody was not performing at the level...they needed to work somewhere else and I made that recommendation (B1).

The "but" introduces the dialectic between the social rule of not firing anybody because of the loyalty Frank had toward his employees and an efficiency rule. Frank's view is expressed by the interviewee using a story, in an extract that I have already cited:

> And then we were at a meeting for a specific individual that has been working at the bank for some period of time and Frank Papen said "no, that person has been with us for a long time", we would keep that person (B1).

And here is a story that shows the interviewee's view:

> But over the years it became obvious that our personnel costs were too high and it was having an adverse effect on profitability but the employees were members of Frank's family (B1).

In these few sentences it can be clearly seen how optimization processes are not always the best solution when alternative and socialized paradigms rule.

Another member faces similar conflict with the loyalty rule:

> I had a lot of struggle with that because my job was to make it work and sometimes you had to make some tough decisions that were inconsistent with that loyalty (C1).

Two different plots are competing, on the one hand is the plotting of family based relations, on the other is the plotting of efficiency and profitability.

Orr's work showed us how "war stories" help solve problems but also constitute a sort of collective memory tank from which the members of the firm draw repertoires of solutions. Orr also focuses his attention on the identity connected with these stories.

We can see in the case of this bank that alternative and competing identities are at play here, suggesting not only different plots but also different genres. Frank's stories are epic stories, stories of great success, like the case in which he was able to move the bank five times, but they are also the stories of a great patriarch that reigned his kingdom. He was not a banker, they always say. The stories of the managers are stories of duty and work, of efficiency and labor.

The decision-making process is an informal process where the exact moment of decision is hardly traceable:

> I will tell you, one of the traditions that had evolved was that before the bank opened and after we would review the rejected checks, after we finished that, we would go to the coffee shop and there was a lot of just general conversation we talked about things happening in the community, things that were happening in sports and happening in politics but you always ended

up to some extends to things that were affecting the bank and that is not to say that we did not have more structured formalized management meetings, but a lot of the conversations, in the coffee shop had to do with banking and a lot of ideas evolved there (A1).

Sometimes decisions are retrospectively created as in the case of Garfinkel's (1967) study of juror deliberations. Garfinkel concentrates on the procedures by which jury members demonstrate that their positions are rational, and this of course is a social process in which jury members participate. Rationality is then seen as a way in which jury members demonstrate and agree upon the social appropriateness of their activities and decisions. The interest in this case is on the socially situated nature of rationality. The emphasis is on "coherence" and "appropriateness", which is ex-post reconstructed.

In place of the view that decisions are made as the occasion require, an alternative formulation needs to be entertained. It consists of the possibility that the person defines retrospectively the decisions that have been made. The outcome comes before the decision [ ] only in retrospect they [jurors] decide what they did that made their decision correct ones [ ] if the above description is accurate, decision making in daily life would thereby have, as a critical feature, the decision maker's task of justifying a course of action [ ] [decision makers] would be much more preoccupied with the problem of assigning outcomes their legitimate history than with question of deciding before the actual occasion of choice the conditions under which one, among a set of alternative possible courses of action, will be elected.

(Garfinkel, 1967, pp. 114–115)

Ex-ante instrumental rationality is then questioned.
Different forms of rationality of economic agents have emerged from different epistemic traditions. The "homo economicus" is at the time treated as "homo sociologicus", or "homo politicus". This basically means that economic action can be seen as social, political or rather psychologically embedded.

In all of the cases there is an attempt to extrapolate the patterns of actions according to interpretative schemas specific to each discipline. Rationality is not really questioned but rather there is an attempt to understand different forms of rationalities.

An interesting position within management studies is that of Nils Brunsson (1985), which states that decision and actions do not share the same roots of rationality. Decision tends to be rational and thus hinders action; action is driven by motivation and commitment, which cannot be explained in terms of rationality. Human actions for Brunsson are driven by irrationality. Brunsson's irrationality is different from garbage can irrationality, which is a form of randomness through which problems, solutions and choice opportunities encounter in manifold ways.

It is relevant to ask oneself if this kind of irrationality is not only a different form of rationality from the economic one, and if ideology considered by Brunsson does not coincide with generic value rationality (and mostly referring to the more strict Parsonian understanding of ideal types rather than Weber's interpretation), returning to the old Weberian distinction between *zweckrational* (end-rational) and *wertrational* (value-rational) actions.

The aim here is not to reconcile empirical understanding of human behavior in terms of rationality as further articulated and emended (Boudon, 1984; Coleman, 1990; Elster, 1986) or enriched with social interaction underpinnings of cultural and symbolic values (Bourdieu, 1972), but rather to open the path of research to both the stabilizing forms of social determinacy and the destabilizing forms of experience. Everyday life, as Jedlowski argues (1994), stands exactly in the midst of these.

This endeavor emphasizes the relational and contextual aspects of action, the sense of which is continuously reinterpreted and not given once for all.

In the interview extracts of the fifth chapter I have shown the ambivalence of human experience, in which both centripetal (toward social order) and centrifugal forces not only coexist but are also necessary for each other. These aspects have been the subject of the previous chapter and are the result of ideas stemming from the phenomenologist tradition (Schütz, 1967), American pragmatism (James, 1907; Rorty 1979), Hermeneutics and Philosophy of Language (Wittgenstein, 1918; Ricoeur, 1981), Post-structuralism

(Foucault, 1966; Derrida, 1967) and Linguistic Pragmatics (Austin, 1962; Searle, 1969; Watzlawick et al., 1967; Bateson, 1972).

It is the idea of "understanding processes from within" which is the title of the argument for "withness" thinking proposed by Shotter (2006) as another way of engaging with reality as opposed to the about process from the outside (Shotter, 2006, p. 586). Of course this supposes the entering into the dialogic.

It is an approach that has solid roots in the philosophical tradition and in the critique of both the purely psychological understanding and the objective and positivistic knowledge. It is deeply connected with the idea of relationality, which has been the object of a recent article by Robert Cooper (2005) in the organization studies domain.

Drawing on all the abovementioned suggestions to the normative understanding of decision-making and on the work done by Chia (1994, 1998a, 1998b) and Cooper (1986, 1989, 2005; Cooper and Burrell, 1988; Cooper and Law, 1995), my proposal a perspective on decision-making that focuses on the everydayness of decisions as decisions happen within our lives, within the flow of events of our lives as "[Decision] cannot be merely constructed as an unproblematic identifiable event out there which we try to locate, uncover, describe and accurately represent because this assumption, this given is itself the outcome of a prior decisional operation" (Chia, 1994, p. 796).

For Chia decisions are better understood as "incisions" in the flow of our phenomenal experience and in this sense comes the work of O'Connor that I have recollected in the second chapter. Cooper (1986) in his organization/disorganization is also concerned with this incisional operation which is the "ontological act of cutting and partitioning off a version of reality from was has hitherto been indistinguishable". Instead of talking about intention and choice these authors insist on the notion of decisional becoming.

Drawing from these critics on the notion of decisions as an unproblematic and unambiguous concept, decision-making can be seen nevertheless as a way to fix meaning, to "construct and reinforce a stable but precarious version of reality" (Chia, 1994), or as Boje puts it "bits and pieces of organization experience are recounted socially throughout the firm to formulate recognizable, cogent, defensible, and seemingly rational collective accounts that will serve as precedent for individual assumption, decision and action" (Boje, 1991).

What I am trying to demonstrate in this chapter is that decision-making can be analyzed on different levels and by using different approaches, as well as narrative. I have presented normative models that deal with optimal decision-making, as in the case of the rational model; descriptive models have provided descriptive insight into how people actually make decisions in organization.

My idea and proposal for future research on decision-making processes is one of escaping from structural understanding of decision-making and the search for connections and patterns of behavior by attempting to incorporate instances that are not yet stabilized but represent nevertheless a guide to understanding the daily life of people involved in decision-making processes.

# Conclusions

In this book I have studied storytelling in organizational contexts. As seen in the first part of the work there has been a growing interest in the last decades on the theme of narrative by organizational scholars. In the second chapter I have outlined some of the work carried out in the field, and I have provided an account of the why and how of such an approach.

Narrative inquiry in organizational research encompasses both the work done using narrative as a methodological approach and the use of concepts of narrative as epistemological and ontological bases. In this work I have used both aspects of the narrative inquiry notion. In the first chapter I have provided an outline of the different interpretations of the notion of narrative provided by literary critics, socio-linguists, philosophers of language and so on. Of course the two levels intertwine as organizational scholars have drawn on such theories to formulate their research questions.

A complex and articulated body of work, only sketched in the first chapter, has produced a galaxy of works in the managerial realm each based on different taxonomies. Structuralist analyses have been paired with socio-constructionist analyses and with postmodern and critical ones to investigate different organizational aspects such as culture, identity, sense-making, problem solving and gender, just to mention a few.

In particular I have considered the work done by Boje, with whom I have conducted the empirical part of my study. Boje has devoted the last 30 years to the study of storytelling in organizations and has become one of the most prolific and refined authors on the subject. His studies on storytelling organizations range from socio-constructionist views in his early work to a critical and postmodern view. Antenarrative is the word he coined to describe his work. Antenarrative is like the word narrative of narrative inquiry, it refers both to an approach, a way of dealing with research, and to a different epistemological foundation of narrative research, which refuses every form of representationalism. Boje shows us how life in organizations is far more complex, chaotic and dialogic than every narrative order would posit.

It is in this line that I have performed my research of an American southwestern banking institution, acquired twice in the last ten years, and now part of a large banking group. The initial idea of studying storytelling and decision-making, has been shaped and evolved through research into a broader interest on the studied organization and its story.

The story of the bank is reconstructed through the accounts of people who have worked for the bank in the past and those of the new comers: by telling the story of the bank these people tell their stories, the stories of their work experiences, their lives inside and outside the bank, in an intricate net of stories already told and yet to be plotted.

In the second part of the book I have given voice to all the different stories that I have collected during my research: the extensive interviews with the bankers, the book written by the historian, the newsletters of the bank, the archival information, the brochures of the new bank and so on.

I have used some of the theory from the first part of the work to comment on such material: the loose definition of narrative with no beginning, middle and end provided by conversational storytelling; the importance of personal experience; the cognitive, instructional, communitarian and identitarian functions of narrative.

A new aspect emerging from the empirical research has been the positive role of storytelling in the creation of a shared collective memory that orally survives in one of the two acquisition processes. But the core of the research must be detected in the emergence of the ambivalence of storytelling acts which witness a constant movement between the consolidated, socially plotted narratives and the rough, unfinished fragments.

In the last part of the book I have shown how different reflections developed within different traditions came together in the consolidated narratives versus rough fragments definition that I provided. They are, in particular, the we-experience/I-experience notion provided by Bakhtin, the *idem/ipse* definition provided by Ricoeur and Jedlowski's common sense/experience reflections.

The sense of the work must be thus sought in the unpredictable, emergent and complex nature of everyday life in organizations. It is also at this level that the antenarrative study of organizations developed by Boje, merges with the study of narrative practices in the everyday life developed by Jedlowski in the perspective of sociology of communication and culture.

Far from this understanding and in the line of a critique is the treatment of narrative and storytelling as an unproblematic and replicable device to achieve efficiency within the organization and recognition outside it.

The open question of the last chapter on decision-making is whether storytelling can be incorporated into the study of particular organizational phenomena such as decision-making using a perspective from "within" and without neglecting the complexity of narrative/antenarrative understanding achieved through the work. The contribution of this work stands exactly in these aspects, that is to say to enter the field of narrative inquiry and to perform narrative research giving voice to the personal and unique experience of the people involved in the process.

As it may be noticed in the work this was not the initial endeavor and the last chapter on decision-making demonstrates that, but it is a sensitivity that has evolved during the research itself and through the contact with both Jedlowski and Boje. It is in this frame that the decision-making loses its centrality; if we want to give voice to experience we have to relax such an a priori concept. As a matter of fact the notion of choice and decision is hardly retraceable in a specific moment of the life of the executives but rather happens in a flow of experience in which the coffee shop talks, the sitting around a table and the speeches of the president inextricably intertwine.

Using the words of a title from Raymond Carver *What We Talk about When We Talk about Love*, we could say "what we talk about when we talk about decisions", to explore the vicissitudes of daily life in organizations. The geography is a human geography of emotions, frustrations, joy and pain in which daily objects such as a clock or the pictures on the wall intertwine with the dry weather of the south west and its exceptional floods, the tower of the bank and much more. Without understanding this sensitivity we can't understand the sense of this work, and its positioning compared to other narrative inquiry researches.

As mentioned in the second chapter, if one would have to compile a synopsis of narrative inquiry in the organizational domain at least four levels of description should be considered: definition of story/narrative; epistemological foundations; methodology and object of study. Of course all these aspects are intertwined but we can't neglect that there are unlimited configurations.

In this book the definition of narrative is relaxed compared to the structuralist understanding, and it is close to the definition provided by Herrnstein Smith of someone telling someone else that something has happened. At this level we neglect the structuralist concern of a passage from one status to another as a minimum requirement of narrative, and the importance given to the plot as an ordering device. Narratives we find in everyday life do not follow this ideal structure: competing narrative plots, interruptions and repetitions are frequent.

In conversational storytelling stories are created in the act of the telling: they are living performances. People organize their accounts in unlimited configurations in which both social embeddedness and personal experience play a primary role. The definition of narrative thus becomes open to the influence of both socio-constructionist views and phenomenological sensitivity. This entails a different understanding of the concept of narrative inquiry and of the techniques of collection of data and analysis.

In this work I have provided no structural interpretation, the narratives are considered for what they represent for the subjects involved in the processes. The notion of antenarrative comes into play both as a way of conducting research and for its ontological value. Together with plotted narratives, locally and socially constructed, we witness the emergence of antenarrative fragments that chase a new order, a new configuration.

The stories are in fact not organized into coherent narratives but remain in some cases at a rough level. It is from this consideration that the articulation of the discussion makes its move, refined through the articulation of the *idem/ipse* distinction of Ricoeur, the I-we experience distinction of Bakhtin and Jedlowski's common sense and experience understanding. It is in the articulation of the distinction between consolidated narratives and rough fragments that the socio-constructionist, phenomenologist and postmodern perspectives meet.

If on the one hand the aspects of social construction of narratives are considered and acknowledged in the work, on the other hand the work aims at showing also the precariousness of such constructions. If storytelling acts as witness to a constant movement between consolidated narratives and rough fragments, the result of the reinscription of personal experience on social accounts is open to infinite endings. However, these endings refer to infinite other stories in a dialogic relation that could never be fully discovered.

# Notes

193

1. For a problematization of the distinction between story and discourse see Culler (1981).
2. I would problematize here the idea of discourse as naive expression of the story according to Hjelmslev's distinction between content and expression (Hjelmslev, 1961).
3. As suggested by Ruggero Eugeni, Professor of Semiotics at the Università Cattolica del Sacro Cuore, Brescia.
4. For further reference see Melucci (2000); Chiaretti, Sebastiani and Rampazi (2001); Di Fraia (2004); Longo (2005).
5. For a problematization of this aspect, see Boje *Living Story Consulting* (forthcoming).
6. On the problematization of determinacy/versus indeterminacy of social action see Crespi (1999).

# References


Allais, R. 1953 Le comportement de l'homme rationnel devant le risque, critique des postulats et axiomes de l'école américaine. *Econometrica*, 21, 503–546.

Allison, G. 1969 *The Essence of Decision. Explaining the Cuban Missile Crisis.* Boston, MA: Little Brown and Company.

Alvesson, M. 2007 Organizations in an age of grandiosity, presentation given at the *Cross-cultural Life of Social Values Conference.* Rotterdam.

Arendt, H. 1985 *The Human Condition.* Chicago: Chicago University Press.

Aristotle, *Physics.*

Augustine, *Confessions.*

Austin, J.L. 1962 *How to do Things with Worlds.* Oxford: Oxford University Press.

Bakhtin, M. 1981 *The Dialogic Imagination: Four essays by M. Bakhtin* (trans. C. Emerson and M. Holoquist). Austin, TX: University of Texas Press.

Bakhtin, M. 1984 *Problems of Dostoevsky's Poetics,* ed. and trans. C.l. Emerson. Minneapolis: University of Minnesota Press.

Bakhtin, M. 1986 *Speech Genres and Other Late Essays,* trans. V.W. McGee. Austin: University of Texas Press.

Bakhtin, M. 1993 *Towards a Philosophy of the Act,* ed. M. Holquist and V. Liapunov. Austin: University of Texas Press.

Bakhtin, M. and Medvedev, P.N. 1978 *Formal Method in Literary Scholarship* (trans. A.C. Wehrle). Baltimore: John Hopkins University Press.

Bakhtin, M. and Volosinov, V.N. 1973 *Marxism and the Philosophy of Language* (trans. L. Matejka and I.R. Titunik). New York: Seminar Press.

Bakhtin, M. and Volosinov, V.N. 1976 *Discourse in Life and Discourse in Art. Concerning Sociological Poetics. In Freudianism. A Marxist critique.* New York: Academic Press.

Baron, J. 1988 *Thinking and Deciding.* Cambridge University Press: Cambridge.

Bateson, G. 1972 *Steps to an Ecology of Mind.* New York: Ballantine Books.

Benjamin, W. 1936 The Storyteller. Reflections on the Works of Nikolai Leskov. In *Illuminations.* New York: Schoken Books, 1969 (ed. Hannah Arendt, trans. Harry Zohn).

Berger, P.L. and Luckmann, T. 1966 *The Social Construction of Reality.* Garden City, NY: Anchor Books.

Bocchi, G. and Ceruti, M. 1985 *La sfida della complessità.* Milano: Feltrinelli.

Boden, D. and Zimmerman, D.H. (eds) 1991 *Talk and Social Structure: Studies in Ethnomethodology and Conversation Analysis.* Cambridge: Polity.

Boje, D. 1991 The Storytelling Organization: A Study of Story Performance in an Office Supply Firm, *Administrative Science Quarterly,* 36 (1), 106–126.

Boje, D. 1995 Stories of the Storytelling Organization: A postmodern Analysis of Disney as Tamara-Land. *Academy of Management Journal*, 38 (4), 997–1035.

Boje, D. 2001 *Narrative Methods for Organizational and Communication Research.* London: Sage.

Boje, D. and Musacchio Adorisio, A.L. 2008 Living Between Myths: Experiences at Wells Fargo Bank. In Monika Kostera (ed.), *Mythical Inspiration for Organizational Realities.* London: Palgrave.

Boudon, R. 1984 *La Place du désordre. Critique des théories du changement social.* Paris: Presses Universitaires de France.

Bourdieu, P. 1972 *Outline of a theory of Practice.* Cambridge: Cambridge University Press.

Bourdieu, P. 1990 *The Logic of Practice.* Cambridge: Polity Press.

Brooks, P. 1984 *Reading for the Plot: Design and Intention in Narrative.* Cambridge, MA: Harvard University Press.

Bruner, J. 1986 *Actual Minds, Possible Worlds.* Cambridge, MA: Harvard University Press.

Brunsson, N. 1985 *The Irrational Organization. Irrationality as a Basis for Organizational Action and Change.* Chichester: John Wiley and Sons.

Camerer, C.F., Loewenstein G. and Rabin, M. 2004 *Advances in Behavioral Economics.* Princeton: Princeton University Press.

Chandler, A.D. 1962 *Strategy and Structure: Chapters in the History of the American Industrial Enterprise.* Cambridge, MA: The MIT Press.

Chia, R. 1994 The Concept of Decision: A Deconstructive Analysis, *Journal of Management Studies*, 31 (6), 781–806.

Chia, R. 1998a *Organized Worlds: Explorations in Technology and Organization with Robert Cooper.* London: Routledge.

Chia, R. 1998b *In the Realm of Organizations: Essays for Robert Cooper.* London: Routledge.

Chiaretti, G., Sebastiani, C. and Rampazi, M. 2001 *Conversazioni, storie, discorsi.* Roma: Carocci.

Clandinin, D.J. (ed.) 2006 *Handbook of Narrative Inquiry: Mapping a Methodology.* Thousand Oaks, CA: Sage.

Clandinin, D.J. and Connelly, F.M. 2000 *Narrative Inquiry. Experiences and Stories in Qualitative Research.* San Francisco: Jossey Bass.

Chatman, S. 1978 *Story and Discourse: Narrative Structure in Fiction and Film.* Ithaca, NY: Cornell University Press.

Chatman, S. 1984 *Reply to Barbara Herrnstein Smith.* In W.J.T. Mitchell (ed.), *On Narrative.* Chicago: The University of Chicago Press.

Clark, B.R. 1972 The Organizational Saga in Higher Education, *Administrative Science Quarterly*, 17, 178–184.

Cohen, M., March, J. and Olsen, J. 1972 A Garbage Can Model of Organizational Choice, *Administrative Science Quarterly*, 17, 1–25.

Coleman, J.S. 1990 *Foundations of Social Theory.* Cambridge: MA: Harvard University Press.

Cooper, R. 1986 Organization/Disorganization, *Social Science Information*, 25, 299–335.

Cooper, R. 1989 Modernism and Postmodernism and Organizational Analysis: the contribution of Jacques Derrida, *Organization Studies*, 10 (4), 479–502.

Cooper, R. 2001 Un-timely mediations: Questioning thought, *Ephemera*, 1 (4), 321–347.

Cooper, R. 2005 Relationality, *Organization Studies*, 26 (11), 1689–1710.

Cooper, R. and Burrell, G. 1988 Modernism, Postmodernism and Organizational Analysis. *Organization Studies*, 9 (1), 91–112.

Cooper, R. and Law, J. 1995 Organization: Distal and Proximal Views. *Research in the Sociology of Organizations*, 13, 237–274.

Crespi, F. 2005 *Sociologia del Linguaggio*. Roma-Bari: Laterza.

Culler, J. 1981 *The Pursuit of Signs, Semiotics, Literature, Deconstruction*. New York: Cornell University Press.

Cyert, R.M. and March, J.G. 1963 *A Behavioral Theory of the Firm*. Englewood Cliffs, NJ: Prentice-Hall.

Czarniawska, B. 1997a *Narrating the Organization. Dramas of Institutional Identity*. Chicago, IL: University of Chicago Press.

Czarniawska, B. 1997b *A Narrative Approach to Organization Studies*. London: Sage.

Czarniawska, B. 1999 *Writing Management. Organization Theory as a Genre*. Oxford: Oxford University Press.

Czarniawska, B. 2004 *Narratives in Social Sciences Research*. London: Sage.

Czarniawska, B. and Gagliardi, P. 2003 *Narratives we organize by*. Amsterdam: John Benjamins.

Denzin, N.K. and Lincoln, Y.S. 1994 *Handbook of Qualitative Research*. Thousand Oaks, CA: Sage.

Di Fraia, G. 2004 *Storie con-fuse. Pensiero narrativo, sociologia e media*. Milano: Angeli, 2004.

Derrida, J. 1967 *De la grammatologie*. Paris: Minuit.

Ellsberg, D. 1961 Risk, Ambuguity and the Savage Axioms, *Quarterly Journal of Economics*, 75, 643–669.

Elster, J. 1986 *Rational Choice*. Oxford: Basil Blackwell.

Fehr, E. and Gachter, S. 2000 Fairness and Retaliation: The Economics of Reciprocity, *Journal of Economic Perspectives*, 14 (3), 159–181.

Feldman M.S. and March, J.G. 1981 Information in Organization as Signal and Symbol. *Administrative Science Quarterly*, 26, 171–186.

Foucault, M. 1966 *Les mots et les choses*. Paris: Gallimard.

Gabriel, Y. 1991 Turning Facts into Stories and Stories into Facts: An Hermeneutic Exploration of Organizational Folklore, *Human Relations*, 44 (8), 857–875.

Gabriel, Y. 2004 *Myths, Stories and Organizations: Postmodern Narratives of our Times*. Oxford: Oxford University Press.

Gadamer, H.G. 1975 *Truth and Method*. London: Sheed and Ward.

Garfinkel, H. 1967 *Studies in Ethnometodology*. Englewood Cliffs, NJ: Prentice Hall.

Genette, G. 1972 *Discours du récit*, in *Figures III*. Paris: Seuil.

Gherardi, S. 2005 *Organizational Knowledge: The Texture of Workplace Learning*, Blackwell: Oxford.

Giddens, A. 1984 *The Constitution of Society*. Berkeley: University of California Press.

Goffman, E. 1959 *The Presentation of Self in Everyday Life*. Edinburgh: University of Edinburgh, Social Sciences Research Centre.

Granovetter, M. 1985 Economic Action and Social Structure: The Problem of Embeddedness, *The American Journal of Sociology*, 91, 481–510.

Güth, W. and Thiez, R. 1990 Ultimatum Bargaining Behavior, *Journal of Economic Psychology*, 11, 417–419.

Halbwachs, M. 1980 *Collective Memory*. New York: Harper and Row.

Herrnstein Smith, B. 1981 *Narrative Versions, Narrative Theories*. In W.T. Mitchell (ed.), *On Narrative*. Chicago: University of Chicago Press.

Hirsh, P.M. 1986 From Ambushes to Golden Parachutes: Corporate Takeovers as an Instance of Cultural Framing and Institutional Integration? *American Journal of Sociology*, 91, 800–837.

Hjelmslev, L. 1961 *Prolegomena to a Theory of Language* (trans. Francis J Whitfield). Madison: University of Wisconsin Press.

James, W. 1907 *Pragmatism: A New Name for Old Ways of Thinking*. New York: Longmans Greens.

Jedlowski, P. 1994 *Il Sapere dell'esperienza*. Milano: Il Saggiatore.

Jedlowski, P. 2000 *Storie Comuni*. Milano: Mondadori.

Jedlowski, P. 2007 L'importanza del destinatario. Pratiche narrative, vita quotidiana, esperienza: uno sguardo sociologico. In G. Marrone, N. Dusi, and G. LoFeudo, (eds), *Narrazione ed Esperienza*. Roma: Meltemi.

Jedlowski, P. 2007 Memoria e interazioni sociali. In E. Agazzi and V. Fortunati (eds), *Memoria e saperi*. Roma: Meltemi.

Jedlowski, P. and Leccardi, C. 2003 *Sociologia della vita quotidiana*. Bologna: Mulino.

Kahneman, D. and Tversky, A. 1979 Prospect Theory: An Analysis of Decision under Risk, *Econometrica*, 47, 263–291.

Kahneman, D., Slovic, P., and Tversky, A. 1982 *Judgment under Uncertainty: Heuristics and Biases*. New York: Cambridge University Press.

Kleindorfer, P.R., Kunreuther, H.C. and Shoemaker, P.J.H. 1993 *Decision Sciences: An Integrative Perspective*. Cambridge: Cambridge University Press.

Koller, V. 2007 The World's Local Bank: Glocalisation as a Strategy in Corporate Branding Discourse, *Social Semiotics*, 17 (1), 111–131.

Lindblom, C. 1959 The Science of Muddling Through. *Public Administration Review*, 19 (2), 79–88.

Longo, M. 2005 Sul racconto in sociologia. Letteratura, senso comune, narrazione sociologica, *Foedus*, 12.

Luce, R.D. and Raiffa, H. 1957 *Games and Decisions*. New York: Wiley.

Lukács, G. 1920 *Die Theorie des Romans*. Berlin: Cassirer.

Lyotard, J.F. 1979 *La Condition Postmoderne*. Paris: Minuit.

MacIntyre, A. 1984 *After Virtue*. Notre Dame: University of Notre Dame Press.

March, J.G. 1978 Bounded Rationality, Ambiguity, and the Engineering of Choice, *Bell Journal of Economics*, 9, 587–608.

March, J.G. 1988 *Decisions and Organizations*. Oxford: Blackwell.

March, J.G. 1994 *A Primer on Decision Making: How Decisions Happen*. New York: The Free Press.

March, J.G. 1997 How Decisions Happen in Organizations. In Zur Shapira (ed.), *Organizational Decision Making*. Cambridge: Cambridge University Press.

March, J.G. and Simon, H.A. 1958 *Organizations*. New York: Wiley.

Marquard, O. 1989 *Farewell to Matter of Principles*. Oxford: Oxford University Press.

Mead, G.H. 1934 *Mind, Self and Society*. Chicago: University of Chicago Press.

Melucci, A. 1998 *Verso una Sociologia Riflessiva*. Bologna: Mulino.

Melucci, A. 2000 Costruzione di sé, narrazione, riconoscimento. In D. Della Porta, M. Greco and A. Szakolczai, A. (eds), *Identità, riconoscimento, scambio*. Roma-Bari: Laterza.

Metz, L. 1991 *Southern New Mexico Empire: The First National Bank of Dona Ana County*. El Paso, Texas: Mangan Books.

Middleton, D. and Edwards, D. 1990 *Collective Remembering*. London: Sage.

Miller, J. and Glassner, B. 2001 The "Inside" and the "Outside": Finding Realities in Interviews. In Silverman, D. (ed.), *Qualitative Research* London: Sage.

Mintzberg, H. and Waters, J.A. 1990 Studying Deciding. *Organization Studies*, 11, 1–16.

Mitroff, I.I. and Killman, R. 1975 Stories Managers Tell: A New Tool for Organizational Problem Solving, *Management Review*, July, 18–28.

Namer, G. 1987 *Mémoire et societé*. Paris: Klincksieck.

von Neumann, J. and Morgenstern, O. 1944 *Theory of Games and Economic Behavior*. Princeton: Princeton University Press.

O'Connor E.S. 1996 Telling Decisions: The Role of Narrative in Organizational Decision Making. In Z. Shapira (ed.), *Organizational Decision Making*, (pp. 304–323). New York: Cambridge University Press.

O'Reilly, C.A., Pfeffer J. and Chang, V. 2004 Wells Fargo and Norwest: "Merger of Equals", *Harvard Business Online*, case HR26B.

Orr, J.E. 1990 Sharing Knowledge, Celebrating Identity: Community Memory in a Service Culture. In D.S. Middleton and D. Edwards (eds), *Collective Remembering: Memory in Society* (pp. 169–189). Beverly Hills: Sage.

Orr, J.E. 1996 *Talking About Machines: An Ethnography of a Modern Job*. Ithaca, NY: Cornell University Press.

Owen, G. 1999 *Las Cruces, New Mexico, 1849–1999. Multicultural Crossroads*. Las Cruces, NM: Red Sky Publishing Co., Inc.

Pettigrew, A. 1990 Studying Deciding, *Organization Studies*, 11, 1–16.

Pfeffer, J. 1981 *Power in Organizations*. Marshfield, MA: Pitman.

Pinnegar, S. and Daynes J.G. 2006 Locating Narrative Inquiry Historically. In Clandinin, D.J. (ed.), *Handbook of Narrative Inquiry: Mapping a Methodology*. Thousand Oaks, CA: Sage.

Porter, M.E. 1979 How Competitive Forces Shape Strategy, *Harvard Business Review*, 57 (2, March-April), 137–145.

Pratt, J.W., Raiffa, H. and Schlaifer, R. 1965 *Introduction to Statistical Decision Theory*. Cambridge, MA: MIT Press.

Priesley, L. 1988 *Shalam – Utopia on the Rio Grande 1881–1907*. El Paso, TX: Texas Western Press.

Prince, G. 1982 *Narratology*. The Hague: Mouton.

Propp, V. 1928 *Morphology of the Folktale*. The Hague: Mouton (1958).

Richardson, L. 1990 Narrative and Sociology, *Journal of Contemporary Ethnography*, 19 (1), 116–135.

Ricoeur, P. 1983 *Time and Narrative*. Baltimore and London: John Hopkins University Press.

Ricoeur, P. 1992 *Oneself as Another*. Chicago: Chicago University Press.

Rorty, R. 1967 *The Linguistic Turn, Essays in Philosophical Method*. Chicago: University of Chicago Press.

Salancik, G. 1977 Commitment and Control of Organizational Behavior and Belief. In B. Staw and G. Salancik (eds), *New Directions in Organizational Behavior* (pp. 1–54) Chicago: St. Clair Press.

Savage, L.J. 1954 *The Foundations of Statistics*. New York: Wiley.

Schafer, R. 1978 *Language and Insight*. New Haven, CT: Yale University Press.

Schafer, R. 1992 *Retelling a Life. Narration and Dialogue in Psychoanalysis*. New York: Basic Books.

Schütz, A. 1967 *The Phenomenology of the Social World*. Evanston: IL: Northwestern University Press.

Searle, J. 1969 *Speech Acts*. Cambridge: Cambridge University Press.

Sennett, R. 1998 *The Corrosion of Character: Personal Consequences of Work in the New Capitalism*. New York: W.W. Norton and Co.

Shafer, G. 1990 *Readings in Uncertain Reasoning* (ed. Judea Pearl). San Mateo, CA: Morgan Kaufmann.

Shotter, J. 2006 Proceedings of the Conference on "Polyphony and Dialogism as a Way of Organizing", 28–30 April, University of Essex, UK.

Shotter, J. 2006 Understanding Process From Within: An Argumentation for "Withness" – Thinking, *Organization Studies*, 27 (4), 585–604.

Šklovskij, V. 1925 *Theory of Prose* (Trans. Benjamin Sher.). Elmwood Park: Dalkey (1990).

Simon, H. 1947 *Administrative Behavior*. New York: MacMillan.

Simon, H. 1957 *Models of Man: Social and Rational*. New York: Wiley.

Smith, A. 1759 *Theory of Moral Sentiments*. London: A. Millar.

Smith, A. 1776 *The Wealth of Nations*. London: Methuen & Co.

Taylor, F. 1947 *The Principles of Scientific Management*. New York: Norton.

Thaler, R. 1980 Toward a Positive Theory of Consumer Choice, *Journal of Economic Behavior and Organisation*, 1, 39–60.

Thaler, R. 1988 The Ultimatum Game, *Journal of Economic Perspectives*, 2 (4), 195–206.

Todorov, T. 1965 *Théorie de la Littérature: Textes des formalistes russes*. Paris: Seuil.

Todorov, T. 1986 Structural Analysis of Narrative. In R.C. Davis (ed.), *Contemporary Literary Criticism: Modernism Through Poststructuralism*. New York: Longman.

Tomaševskij, B. 1975 *Teoria della letteratura*. Milano: Bompiani.

Tversky, A. and Kahneman, D. 1974 Judgment Under Uncertainty: Heuristics and Biases, *Science*, 185 (4157), 1124–1131.

Tversky, A. and Kahneman, D. 1992 Advances in Prospect Theory: Cumulative Representation of Uncertainty, *Journal of Risk and Uncertainty*, 5 (November), 297–323.

Vattimo, G. 1998 *The End of Modernity. Nihilism and Hermeneutics in Postmodern Culture*. Cambridge: Polity Press.

Wald, A. 1939 Contributions to the Theory of Statistical Estimation and Testing Hypothesis, *Annals of Mathematical Statistics*, 10 (4 December), 299–326.

Wallas, G. 1926 *The Art of Though*. New York: Harcourt Brace.

Warglien, M. and Masuch, M. 1996 *The Logic of Organizational Disorder*. Berlin, New York: Walter de Gruyter.

Watzlawick, P., Beavin, G.H. and Jackson, D.D. 1967 *Pragmatics of Human Communication*. New York: W.W. Norton & Co.

Westwood, R. and Linstead, S. 2001 *The Language of Organization*. London: Sage.

Weick, K. 1969 *The Social Psychology of Organizing*. Reading, MA: Addison-Wesley.

Weick, K. 1994 *Sensemaking in Organizations*. Thousand Oaks, CA: Sage.

Wittgenstein, L. 1918 *Tractatus Logico-Philosophicus*. London: Routledge and Kegan Paul.

Wittgenstein, L. 1958 *Philosophical Investigations* (eds. G.E.M. Anscombe and R. Rhees, trans. G.E.M. Ascombe). Oxford: Blackwell.

## Films

Robert Altman, *Nashville* (1975); *Short Cuts* (1993); *Prairie Home Companion* (2006).

Akira Kurosawa, *Rashomon*, 1950.

Gaspar Noé, *Irréversible*, 2002.

Quentin Tarantino, *Pulp Fiction*, 1994.

## Fiction

Boccaccio, *Decameron. One Thousand and One Night*, 1349–1351.

Tolstoj, Lev, *Anna Karenina*, 1877.

Joyce, James, *Dubliners*, 1914.

Eco, Umberto, *Il Nome della Rosa*, 1980.

Calvino, Italo, *Se una notte d'inverno un viaggiatore*, 1979.

## Dictionaries

Micro, Robert, 2003.

The New Oxford Dictionary of English, 2003.

## Websites

http://en.wikipedia.org/wiki/Wells_Fargo
http://www.amazon.com/Stagecoach-Wells-Fargo-American-West/
    dp/product-description/0743234367
www.reference.com/browse/wiki/Wells_Fargo
http://en.wikipedia.org/wiki/Richard_Kovacevich

# Index

Acosta, Manuel, 92
acquisitions, Las Cruces bank, 72,
    113–18
    First National Bank by First
        Security Corporation, 113
    First Security Corporation by Wells
        Fargo, 113
    historical feature, mergers as, 114
    Norwest and Wells Fargo, merger,
        113–14
    Wells Fargo acquisition from First
        National Bank, 114
acts, storytelling acts, 30, 148,
    150–1, 154, 158
    I–We poles of, 150–1, 158–60
    re-inscription of I–We poles, 151,
        154, 158–60
*Administrative Behavior*, 166
*Administrative Science* article, 37
Allison, G., 170
alternative mode of knowing, 15–17
Altman, Robert, 14
*Anna Karenina*, 9
antenarratives, 3, 15, 30, 46, 71, 150,
    158, 165, 189–91
    Boje's concept, 15, 30, 46, 116,
        139, 150, 159, 180, 190;
        definition, 158
'Anthony story', 83–4, 152
Arendt, H., 11, 151
Aristotle, 13
Arrow-Debreu general-equilibrium
    theory, 169
Augustine, 13
Austin, J. L., 16, 23

Bakhtin, M., xi, 2–3, 11, 14, 23–4,
    28, 46, 47, 145–6, 147–9, 190–91
Bateson, G., 24
Bayesian decision theory, 166
Beavin, G. H., 24

beginning, Las Cruces bank, 72, 75–7
    consolidated narratives, 76
    conversational storytelling, 75–7
    as First National Bank of Las
        Cruces, 76
    ninetieth anniversary, 77
    origins of the bank, 75
behavioral decision theory, 165,
    171–4
    main streams of research in, 172
Benjamin, W., 10, 25, 112–13
Benveniste, French linguist, 23
Berger, P. L., 180
biases, 172–3
Boccaccio, 9
Bocchi, G., 18
Boden, D., 69
Boje, D., 1, 15, 30, 32, 37–9, 48–9,
    54–7, 60–2, 65, 68, 71, 80, 91,
    126, 138–9, 150, 158, 160, 186,
    188, 190, 193
bounded rationality, 168–71, 173
Bourdieu, P., 30
Brooks, P., 18–20
Brunsson, N., 185

Calvino, Italo, 21
Carver, Raymond, 190
centrifugal forces of language,
    14, 185
centripetal forces of language,
    14, 185
Ceruti, M., 18
Chang, V., 114
Chatman, S., 8, 11
Chia, R., 186
Chiaretti, G., 193n4
Clandinin, D. J., 29, 47
Clark, B. R., 31, 48
cognitive function of storytelling,
    35–6, 106, 146, 154–5, 157–9,
    164, 169, 189